1974

Home Repairs *Any* Woman Can Do

by

TOM PHILBIN

PRENTICE - HALL, INC.
Englewood Cliffs, N. J.

Home Repairs Any *Woman Can Do*
by Tom Philbin
Copyright © 1973 by Tom Philbin
Printed in the United States of America
Prentice-Hall International, Inc., London
Prentice-Hall of Australia, Pty. Ltd., North Sydney
Prentice-Hall of Canada, Ltd., Toronto
Prentice-Hall of India Private Ltd., New Delhi
Prentice-Hall of Japan, Inc., Tokyo
10 9 8 7 6 5 4 3 2 1

Library of Congress Cataloging in Publication Data
Philbin, Tom
    Home repairs any woman can do.
1. Dwellings—Maintenance and repair. I. Title.
TH4817.P45   643'.7   72-8625
ISBN 0-13-395038-7

CREDITS: One photograph courtesy Red Devil, Inc.
All other photographs by John Capotosto
Drawings by John Savage

Introduction

This is a pretty short book, but I think it will save you lots of money—time and again. In fact, I'm betting that the first time you use it, you'll say it's worth a heck of a lot more than the price. Indeed, if you were to use it only to fix a leaky faucet, you'd save around $15, based on going plumbers' rates.

This book has been a labor of love—and sweat—for me. I've striven to select repairs that I think the average woman can handle, both physically and in terms of mechanical complexity. Above all, I've tried to write in clear, down-to-earth language, avoiding technical gobbledy-gook; an aperture is an aperture, but it's also a hole and that's what I've called it. A constant image kept coming to me as I wrote: a woman, alone in her home, faced with a fix-up problem and only this book to enable her to solve it. Believe me, that image was a cruel taskmaster.

Where helpful, I've given brand names of necessary repair products and a good idea of costs. Your hardware store dealer or other supplier will know exactly what you want. And you'll know what you should pay.

If you're like the average woman—or man—you're probably a little leery about making home repairs. But I think you'll discover, as you read the book, that there's really nothing to be afraid of. Once you *know how* to make repairs, you'll realize that it's no big deal.

Good reading—and repairing!

Tom Philbin
New York, N.Y.

Contents

Contents

8: Miscellaneous Maladies   126

1

Plumbing Problems

Dripping Faucet

This is one of the most common problems around the home. But it is definitely not something you need call the plumber for. The repair will likely take all of five minutes and cost a grand total of 10¢ or so.

Of course, the time you're most likely to notice a dripping faucet is in the middle of the night, when the house is quiet. And that's no time to repair anything.

You needn't. You can silence the drip temporarily and make the repair in the morning. To do this, find a long piece of string, or a shoelace. Wet the string thoroughly, then tie one end of it to the faucet nozzle, letting the rest hang down into the drain. Fiddle with the tied-on end until the dripping water runs down the string. This will carry it silently to the drain. That's it. If you don't have a piece of string, use a rag or sock or towel. First, of course, wet it thoroughly.

To make the repair, you should know how a faucet

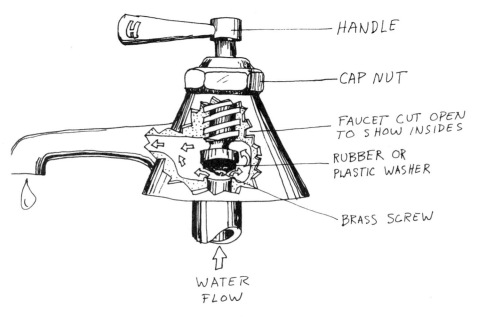

A faucet is basically a simple device for controlling water flow.
Water comes up through the hole in the faucet. When the handle is
turned off, the washer presses against the hole and won't let the
water out. When the handle is turned on, as it is here, the washer lifts
off the hole and the water flows.

works. The handle of the faucet is attached to a shaft,
called a spindle, with a threaded part that screws down
against and covers a hole inside the faucet body—the part
that's attached to the sink. Water is constantly being fed
through pipes to the faucet, but when the faucet is off,
the bottom of the spindle acts like a cork—water pushes
against it but can't get out. When you turn the faucet on,
the spindle screws up out of the hole and water flows.

The thing that really seals off the hole is the washer
on the bottom of the spindle. This is a rubber or fiber device shaped like a little black doughnut. It's soft, and

makes a good sealer to prevent the water from slipping
out past the edges of the spindle. With time, however,
this washer wears out, or loses its shape. Then it doesn't
seal off the water completely. Just a little gets by, and
you get the drip-drip-drip.

Your first inclination is to turn the faucet tighter.
And this will stop the drip temporarily, because the washer will press more tightly in the hole. But ultimately—in
a day or two or a week—the washer will become so worn
that you'll get a drip no matter how tightly you turn off
the faucet.

To make the repair, simply replace the washer. To do
this, you need to take apart the faucet. First, though,
turn off the water supply going to the dripping faucet.

How do you do this? You turn off the pipe valve; it
looks like a little spoked wheel. In most homes, the valve
will be located under the sink. There will be two, one for
the hot water and one for the cold. Feel the pipes. The
one that is warm will be the hot water pipe; the cold one
will be for the cold water. When you locate the right valve,
turn it off by turning it to the right as tightly as you can.

Of course this can be confusing—there may be a number of valves under there. If this is the case, and you're
not sure which one to turn, just turn off all the valves
you can see. No harm done. But first turn on both faucets. When you turn the right valve off, the water will
stop.

In some homes you won't see any valves under the
sink at all. Look on the walls—any valves there? If all else
fails, you can turn off the main valve. This will be located
right next to the water meter on the main pipe—a pipe

that brings all the water into your house. The valve will
be on the left side of the pipe. Turn it to the right. If you
aren't sure where the main valve is, call your water company. They'll know—or have someone come over and
show you.

   Taking the faucet apart will depend on what kind
you have. But taking any apart is all basically the same.
You unscrew or turn the things that look like they can
be unscrewed or turned and the faucet comes apart.
There's no great mystery involved.

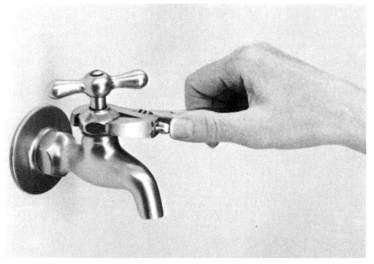

A faucet with a big fat nut on the outside is even easier to take apart.
Just slip a wrench or pliers over the nut and turn it to the left. Then
turn the faucet handle round and round until the spindle comes up
and out.

   One common type has the faucet shaft, or spindle,
held on the faucet body by a big chrome nut. Obtain an
adjustable wrench (one for $2 or $3 at Sears will be good
enough), with jaws that open at least 1 inch wide—or any

When you replace the spindle, if the handle is not in the same position as the other one, take off the screw holding it on, then place
the handle in the proper position and retighten the screw.

type of wrench with jaws that open that wide. Pliers can
also be used. Wrap Band-Aids or tape around the chrome
nut to protect its shiny finish, then place the jaws of the
wrench on the nut, tighten them up, and turn counterclockwise—to the left. After a few turns, you should be
able to turn the nut by hand. Loosen it all the way, then
turn the faucet handle in the "On" direction until the
whole shaft comes up and out of the faucet body.

At the bottom of the shaft, as mentioned, is the
washer, held on by a tiny screw. Take the little screw off
with a screwdriver and remove the washer. On some
shafts, you can lift it right off. Others will have to be
pried a little with the point of a knife.

Take the old washer and screw down to your dealer
and ask him for ones just like them—the same size and
shape. The cost will be about 10¢. Make sure you get a

brass screw—not one that's colored to look like brass.
Pure brass won't corrode; steel ones will. To make absolutely sure it's brass, if your dealer is not, try picking up
the screw with a magnet. If you can't pick it up, that's
good—brass can't be picked up with a magnet. Steel, however, can.

Place the new washer on, insert the little screw, and
tighten. Then just screw the shaft down into the faucet
body and tighten the big fat nut. Do it slowly, don't
force, and keep the shaft and nut straight as you do.
That's it.

Another common type of faucet has no big fat nut
on the outside. The handle covers the shaft, or spindle.
So, remove the handle. You do this by unscrewing the so-
called Phillips screw that holds it on. This is a screw with
crisscross slots rather than just one slot.

Any faucet can be taken apart, no matter how complicated it looks.
On the one shown here, the first step is to take off the so-called
Phillips screw that holds on the handle. Do this with a medium-sized
Phillips screwdriver or the tip of a butter knife.

Lift the handle off (you may have to pry upwards a little). Inside you'll see a nut like the one the finger is pointing to.

Loosen the nut with an adjustable wrench or a pair of pliers by turning it to the left. Then slip the handle over the top of the shaft (spindle) and turn it as if you were turning the faucet on.

The spindle will unscrew up and out. On the bottom will be the
washer, held on by a little screw.

When the screw is off, tap and pry or simply lift up
the handle to get it off.

With the handle off, you'll see a big nut inside. Just
turn this counterclockwise until loose. Then put the handle back over the top of the shaft and turn it as if you
were turning the faucet on. The whole thing will come up
and out. On the bottom, of course, you'll see the washer.

Not so incidentally, you may have trouble turning
the screw that holds the washer on—especially if it's
steel. It gets rusted and corroded. If you have trouble,
buy a little can of penetrating oil (the cost is around 40¢).
Put a few drops on the screw. Give the oil five minutes to
seep down in around the threads of the screw. Then turn.
It should come free. If not, try a little more oil. (Oil also
works in loosening any other type of nut.)

If you turn the screw so hard in trying to free it that
you break the head off, the problem can also be solved.
Use a screwdriver or nail file or some such to dig out the

washer. Apply a few drops of oil on the screw. Wait five minutes, then grip the headless screw with a pair of pliers and turn it out.

If replacing the washer doesn't solve the problem, it means that some metal part inside the faucet is worn out, and repairing it is a job for a plumber, or someone familiar with the problems. But it is highly likely that the new washer will fix things.

One other thing. Once you've repaired a leaking faucet you'll know where the valve is that controls water flow. So if the faucet starts dripping in the middle of the night, turning off the valve will stop the drip. Of course, you still may want to use the string-on-faucet trick if turning off the water means going down in the basement. That's no place to go at such an hour.

Dribbling Faucet

This is far less common than a dripping faucet, but can occur when faucets have the big fat nut on the outside. Namely, water dribbles out around the top of the big nut.

This may be simply because the nut is not tight enough. No need to turn off the water. Just turn the nut a little more to the right to tighten it.

If this doesn't solve the problem, it means the packing—the graphite-soaked "string" that seals off water from getting out past the big nut—is worn out.

Turn off the water and take the faucet apart. Look under the big fat nut. See the packing? Take it out and discard it. Obtain a small package of packing (it costs about 10¢) at the hardware store. Hold one end on the

When water dribbles out around the top of the big fat nut, it means that either the nut is not on tight enough or the packing—the graphite-soaked string—under the nut is worn out.

shaft under the big nut and wrap the packing four or five times around the shaft. Cut off the rest.

Put the faucet back together. Turn the faucet on. Does the water still dribble out around the top of the big nut? If so, add more packing.

Some modern faucets don't have packing—they have what is called an O ring. It's just a big ring of rubber that replaces the packing. If you find one of these, take it down to your dealer and get one just like it.

Stopped-Up Sink

When a kitchen, bathroom, or other sink becomes stopped up or the water drains slowly, you can try a number of things to get the water flowing again.

First, carefully reach down through the water (a knife or other sharp object may be lying in wait) and feel around the drain strainer. Sometimes lint, soap scum, food, or the like can collect quickly and clog things up. Pick out whatever you can with your fingers. After the water drains, remove anything else you can see. For this, a pair of tweezers may come in handy.

If this doesn't get the water flowing, try the next thing, the plunger. You've probably seen one of these. It consists of a handle that looks like a sawed-in-half broomstick on one end of which is a rubber cup.

You may be able to borrow a plunger. But buying one is a good investment. I recommend one that is good for clearing both sink and toilet blockages. The cup has a little bulb on it that fits snugly into the hole in the toilet. To use it on a sink, you snap the bulb inside the cup. At any rate, get a hefty one—six inches in diameter. Sears has a good one for under $3.

The plunger works by getting the water lying in the pipe to move back and forth, alternately pushing against the blockage and sucking it upward, and thus working it free.

To use the plunger, first make sure the sink has at least six inches of water in it. If the blocked water is not six inches deep, run some more in. This is to insure that the plunger cup is under water at all times while you're plunging.

Place the cup over the drain and push down hard, compressing the plunger, then jerk up so the cup lifts off the drain about a half inch. Push down again, lift off, and continue like this, trying to keep a nice, steady rhythm. Keep the bottom of the plunger under water at all times.

Every 30 seconds or so, jerk up extra hard and check to see if the water is going down. If it is, continue plung-

When a sink is stopped up, try plunging it first. Fill the sink so the plunger is covered with water. Press the plunger down on the drain, then lift up about a half inch or so. Repeat in a steady rhythm, every now and then pulling up hard on the plunger.

ing until it is all gone. Then turn on the faucet full blast to see if the water goes down freely. It it does, this means that the blockage has been knocked loose and is heading for the sewer line. As a final treatment, turn on the hot water for a few minutes.

Not so incidentally, if the sink has a little overflow outlet (this will be above the drain on the back side of the sink), this must be plugged with a sopping wet rag while you plunge. Or if you're plunging one of a pair of sinks, you must plug the other sink's drain. Of course, you'll need a helper. If you don't plug that other opening, the suction you're creating by plunging will escape— you won't get much result.

If the plunger doesn't do the job after five minutes or so, call it quits. You'll be ready to, because plunging is hard work.

The next step in that case, is to clean out the so-called

"trap." This is a U-shaped section of pipe directly under the sink. Its purpose is to trap a little water that in turn serves as a seal to prevent sewer gas from backing up the drain pipe and out the drain. But the trap is also a perfect place for things like knives, forks, toothbrushes, spoons, rings—you name it—to collect and eventually block the water.

Some traps have a plug at the very bottom. Place a pan or pail under this plug and use a wrench or pliers to turn the plug counterclockwise to loosen it, then unscrew it with your fingers. When you do, it's likely that whatever was causing the blockage—plus the water in the sink —will plop down into the pan or pail.

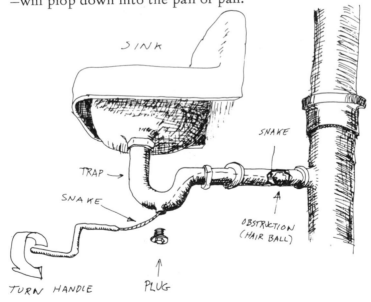

When the plunger doesn't work, take off the plug on bottom of the "trap." The blockage may pass out. If it doesn't, it means the blockage is further in the pipe. Push the snake in, turning it as you push, to try and force the blockage out.

Some traps don't have plugs in them. If this is the case, take a wrench and loosen each of the big nuts that are at the top ends of the "U." Slip these nuts up and off the U and, gently, rock it back and forth until you can take it out. If something is wedged inside it, poke inside with a piece of hanger wire. Then put back the pipe and tighten the nuts. Make sure you get them on straight.

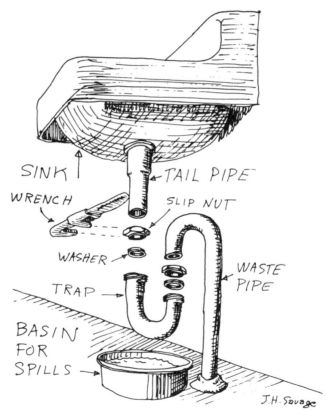

Some sinks don't have trap plugs. You must remove the entire trap. Loosen the two nuts shown.

Whenever you clean out a trap—one with or without a plug—always finish the job by letting the hot water run for five minutes. This will clear away any grease deposits that might have collected where the blockage was.

Your final try to clear the blockage is with the "snake." This is a flexible wire cable with a point on one end and a tube-like handle on the other. Snakes come in various lengths. One about 8 feet long is good enough. To get quality, pay $2 or so for it. As with a plunger, it doesn't pay to buy a puny tool.

First, take off the trap plug, or the trap itself. With your hands, feed the snake into the pipe that goes into the wall. When it's firmly implanted, slide the tube-like handle down along the cable until it is a couple of feet from the pipe opening and lock it in place by turning the little screw on it. Then push the snake in, at the same time turning the tube handle, which will turn the snake.

If the snake becomes stuck, it may just mean that it's ensnarled in a bend in the pipe. On the other hand, you may have located the blockage. Push and pull and twist. If it feels like it's really stuck, pull it all the way out. The little hooked end may have caught on the blockage and you may be able to drag it out. If not, start all over again.

As you feed the snake into the pipe, keep sliding the handle down and setting it in position. If the blockage still is not cleared when you've fed all of the snake in that you can, it's time to call the plumber. The blockage is either wedged in too hard and requires bigger equipment to clear it, or it is located beyond the reach of your snake.

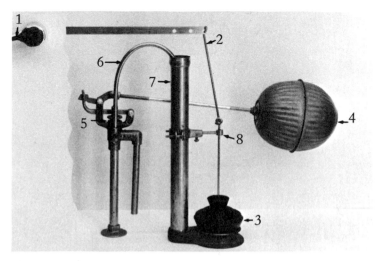

This cutaway view shows the inside of a toilet tank. It looks complicated, but isn't. See the text for how it works.

Toilet Doesn't Stop Running

Problems with a toilet usually occur because something goes wrong in the flush tank—the squarish box
above the toilet, which holds the flush water.

It's a good idea to get thoroughly familiar with how
a toilet works before doing any repairs. So carry this
book into the bathroom and let's check it out. Also, re-
fer to the numbered drawing on this page as we go along.

First, lift off the top of the tank. Do this carefully. If
you drop it, it could chip or break.

Set it aside and look down into the tank. Looks like
a hopeless jungle of piping, doesn't it? It's really not complicated.

Turn the tank handle (1) just a little. When you do,
you'll see that it moves a vertical rod (or chain), number
2 in the photo, upward a little.

Okay, turn the handle fully to flush the tank. See

what happens? The rod (or chain) lifts a rubber ball (3) that's resting in a hole in the bottom of the tank. When the ball is lifted out of the hole, the water in the tank runs out into the bowl, flushing it. Then the tank fills up again, automatically.

Flush the tank again and watch what happens to part number 4, the float. As the water runs out, the float—which of course is floating—goes down with the water level.

This float does two jobs. First, when it gets near the bottom of the tank, the end of the rod it's on opens up number 5—called a water inlet valve—and new water starts to rush into the tank. At the same time, the ball at the bottom of the tank, which has been held up by water rushing past it through the hole, drops down and closes the hole, because there's no more water to keep it open. Second, as the water level rises, the float rises, and the end of the rod it's on gradually closes off the water inlet valve. So the float turns the water on and off.

While the tank is filling, a little tube (6) shoots water into the overflow tube (7) and fills up the bowl itself. If for some reason the incoming water flow is not shut off, the water will flow out the overflow tube into the bowl. There is no way that a toilet tank can overflow.

There are other parts to a toilet tank mechanism, but knowing those mentioned will enable you to make the majority of the repairs required.

Now, let's cover the common problems.

First, if you have a problem, take off the tank top so you can see what is going on.

If, after flushing, water keeps on running into the

bowl and yet the tank doesn't fill up all the way, it usually means that the little rubber ball at the bottom of the tank is defective. What's happening is that it is not plugging up the hole completely.

The cure is to replace the ball. First, shut off the water to the tank. This is done by turning off the water supply to the tank. You can do this by turning off the valve (little wheel) either below the tank or somewhere on the bathroom wall. An easier way, however, is by simply lifting the rod that the float is on as high as you can, then tying it in that position to something above the tank (like a cabinet door knob). As you may remember, this closes off the inlet water valve.

Flush the tank, emptying it. When it's empty, hold the rod (or chain) that the ball is on and unscrew the ball with the other hand. Place it aside and gently wipe off the edges of the hole the ball rests in with a clump of fine-grade steel wool (available at hardware stores).

Sometimes a toilet will continue to run because the hole the ball sits in is clogged with dirt and the ball's fit is not watertight. Clean out the seat for the ball with fine-grade steel wool.

Take the ball down to your local hardware store and ask for one just like it. If, when you took the ball off, you noticed that the rod it was attached to was bent, get a new one of those, too. A bent rod can keep the ball from going in straight and plugging the hole completely.

With the rod in place, screw the new ball onto it. Untie the float rod or turn the water supply valve back on. Flush the toilet. If the water still runs out of the tank and the tank doesn't fill all the way, the ball is not fitting into the hole properly. This can be because the little

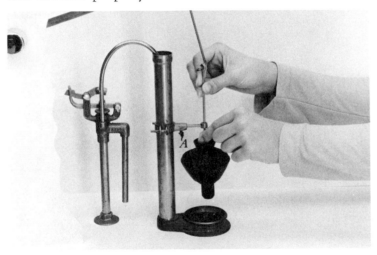

The guide rod must hold the ball straight in the hole or the tank will continually leak. Loosening the little screw (A) will enable you to move the arm that controls the position of the guide.

guide arm (8) that the rod fits through may not be properly positioned. Just turn off the water supply again, then loosen the little screw holding the arm to the overflow tube and jiggle the arm back and forth until the ball drops into the hole perfectly. Then tighten the screw to hold the rod permanently in that position.

Both the rod and the float unscrew easily if you have to replace them.

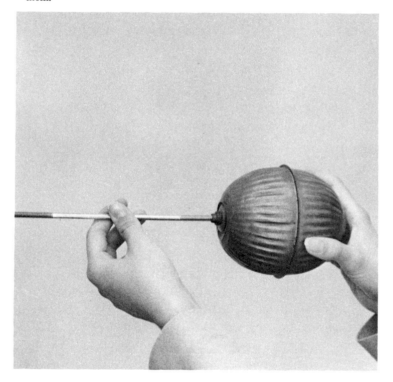

Another problem is that the tank fills up all the way but the water continues to run until it goes out the overflow tube. If this is happening, you'll not only see the water running out the overflow pipe but hear a hissing noise. Something is wrong with either the water inlet valve or the float or its particular rod.

Lift up the float. If the hissing noise stops and the water stops flowing, it means the trouble is with the float or the rod.

Flush the toilet, emptying the tank. Tie the rod as before to shut off the water, or turn it off by turning off the water supply valve.

Unscrew the float and shake it. If there is water inside, the float must be replaced. Simply trot down to your local hardware store and get one just like it (about 25¢). Screw the new float in place, untie the rod (or turn the water supply valve on), and flush the tank. The tank should fill up but not overflow.

If you find when you take off the float that it doesn't have water in it, the problem is with the rod that it is on. To correct this, screw the rod in tightly and then simply bend the rod downwards with your hands, so the float is another half inch or so down into the tank. Flush the toilet. The float should be positioned so the water stops about an inch from the top of the overflow pipe. If it doesn't, bend the rod a little more to achieve this.

If your first test of lifting the rod up does not shut off the water flow, it means that something is wrong with the water inlet valve. Fixing this is a job for a plumber.

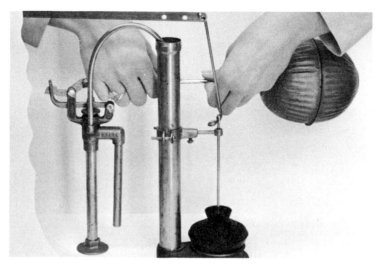

If water keeps running out of the overflow tube, bending down the float rod may cure it.

Stopped-Up Toilet

Solving this problem is similar to handling a stopped-up drain. However, when water starts to rise in the bowl, the first thing to know is how to turn off the water going into it.

The quickest way is to lift up the rod that the float is on; this is explained in the "Toilet Doesn't Stop Running" section. Just take off the top of the flush tank, grab the rod, and pull up—this stops the water. Then tie the rod to the nearest cabinet knob or something else to hold it in position.

The first thing to use to clear the blockage is a plunger. Best kind to get is the two-way force cup, mentioned in the stopped-up sink section. This has a bulb on the end of the rubber cup, which fits snugly into the hole at the bottom of the bowl. When you plunge you get better suction. A six-inch-diameter one will be good.

A plunger usually works when a toilet is stopped up. Just push up and down in a steady rhythm, occasionally pulling up hard. You'll feel suction if you're doing it right.

Plunge the bowl as you would a sink. Place the plunger bulb into the hole at the bottom and press forcefully down on the plunger, compressing it. Pull up about an inch, then press down again. Go up and down in a steady rhythm, every now and then pulling up hard. If you see the water starting to go down, continue to plunge until it is all gone. As a final test to see if the blockage is cleared, flush the toilet. Be ready to grab the rod to stop the water flow in case the blockage isn't gone.

If, before you start to plunge, the bowl is filled to the brim with water, take an old pot or pail and ladle out some of it, say six inches. Otherwise, when you start to plunge, the water will spill on the floor.

If five minutes of plunging doesn't do the trick, you have to take sterner measures. The name of the game here is the closet auger, a "snake" that is especially designed for clearing toilet blockages. It gets its name from "water closet."

A closet auger is like the snake described in the stopped-up sink section, being a wire with a pointy end, but it is thicker and less flexible and it has a crank handle.

Closet augers are sold in various sizes. One six feet long will be good. Sears sells them for under $3.50.

To use the auger, feed the end in with your hands. When it's inside the hole, push it upward. As you can see in the sketch, the end has to get over a hump-like part just beyond the hole in order for it to get to the drain pipe.

Keep pushing it in with your hands. When enough of it is in so you can push it with the handle, do so, at the same time cranking it. This will turn the end of the auger.

If the auger becomes stuck, it may mean that you've contacted the blockage. Push extra hard, also turning. If it feels as though the point on the end of the auger has caught on something, pull out hard. You could drag the thing out.

Of course, it could also mean that the auger is wedged into a pipe bend. Anyway, just keep pushing and turning until all of the auger has disappeared. If the toilet still isn't clear, its a job for a plumber.

Clogged Faucet Strainer

Many faucets are equipped with a little strainer-like device that screws onto the end of the faucet. Its purpose is to aerate the water so it doesn't splash when it hits the sink. When one of these gets clogged with soil, the water starts to jet—and splash—rather than flowing in a soft, smooth stream.

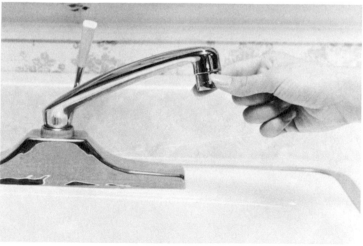

If a faucet strainer is clogged, remove it by unscrewing it to the left. If necessary, use a wrench or pliers.

To cure the problem, first remove the device from the faucet. Sometimes you can do this by simply turning it to the left or right—whichever way the thing goes—with your fingers. If necessary, use a pair of pliers, first wrapping a little tape around the device to protect its shiny finish from the jaws of the pliers.

Remove the little screens (or screen) from the device. You can poke them out with your finger or pick them out with the point of a knife. Note where each goes, so you can reassemble them properly later. (Some screens may not come out, so just brush the exposed screen vigorously. That usually does the trick.)

Using an old toothbrush and a little hand soap, brush the screens thoroughly, even if dirt isn't visible. Rinse them thoroughly, replace them, and then screw the device back onto the faucet and tighten carefully.

Brush screens (or screen) vigorously with an old toothbrush, even if you can't see soil.

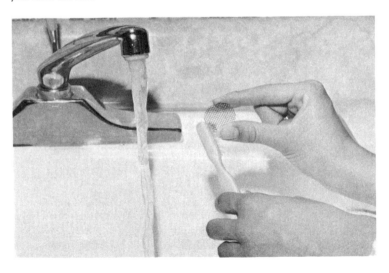

Erratic Shower Spray

If the shower head ejects water in a hard stream, it probably means that inside is a buildup of scale and soil. Some of the little holes where the water comes out are clogged; so the water is virtually fired out of the other ones.

First, grip the shower head in your hand and turn it counterclockwise. It should come right off. If you need help, use a wrench or pliers.

Using a flashlight, look down into the hole in the back of the head. You'll likely see some foreign matter. If you hold the head to the light, you'll see that some of the holes are blocked.

Soap up a Q-Tip, or a toothpick with cotton on the end, and work down inside the shower head, clearing the holes and wiping the entire inside of the head. After a few minutes discard the Q-Tip and run hot water through the hole in the head so it emerges from the little holes. Repeat the procedure four or five times until a Q-Tip emerges as clean as it went in.

Screw the head back on the shower and turn on the water. If it doesn't come out properly, repeat the Q-Tip procedure as needed.

Leaky Pipes

You may be surprised to know that you can probably repair a leaky pipe. Not one that's spewing water—that's a job for a plumber—but the pinhole or small-hole leaks that drip or even spray a fairly steady stream of water.

The first thing to do is to turn off the water. As with a faucet, there are valves controlling water flow through particular pipes; ideally, you'd simply turn off the valve

that would stop water flowing through the damaged pipe.
If you're not sure which valve controls what, you can
turn off the main water valve, as described under "Dripping Faucet." As you know, however, this will turn off
both hot and cold water everywhere in the house.

The repair can be made in a variety of ways.

One way is with an epoxy putty, such as Devcon
Epoxy Adhesive and Filler. The ten-ounce size costs
about $1.75.

To use it, first wipe the damaged area of the pipe absolutely dry. Clean it by rubbing briskly with steel wool.
Then, following label directions, mix the two-part adhe-
sive/filler together and swab it onto and around the hole.

That's it, but the material does take ten or more

A bad leaky pipe is a job for a plumber. But a ready-made patch
and clamp will temporarily stop a small leak. Place the rubber on
pipe, position the clamp over it . . .

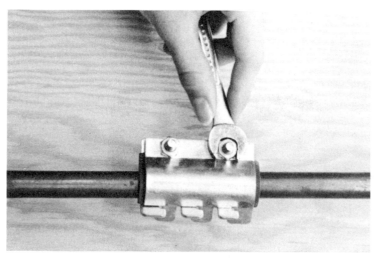

... And tighten the clamp.

hours to dry. It is obviously impractical if you have to turn off the main water valve.

Better, if you are going to turn off the main valve, is a clamp-type patch obtainable at hardware stores. It comes with a rubber patch that looks like a bicycle tube patch. Place this patch over the hole, then slip the clamp device over the patch; tighten the clamp with the bolts provided. This presses the rubber hard against the hole, and water can't get out. You can turn the water on right away; it's a five-minute repair.

Both of these repairs—the epoxy and the clamp—will last indefinitely.

For a hole in a drain pipe under the sink, you can make a quick repair with aluminum tape, such as the Arno Company makes. First wipe the pipe dry. Peel off the paper backing on the tape and tightly wrap the pipe. If the leak is near a joint, you can form the tape with your fingers so it fits snugly.

2

Furniture Scratches and Stains

Furniture Scratches and Stains

Furniture, especially wood furniture, is subject to attack from budding Michelangelos with ball-point pens (including at least one little girl I know who scratched her name in the top of a TV) to guests who have no appreciation of the fact that wet glasses can leave rings. At any rate, a variety of problems can occur. Following is a roundup of these problems—with solutions. It should be emphasized that some damage cannot be handled so it is absolutely invisible—only complete refinishing might do that. However, you can repair a blemish to the point where only the closest possible inspection will reveal it.

Scratches

These can be either shallow or deep. If they've penetrated the finish—varnish, shellac, lacquer, or a combination of these—and exposed raw wood, they are classified as deep. If they haven't, they're shallow.

A shallow scratch on red mahogany furniture can sometimes be hidden by applying a little ordinary iodine.

If the scratch is shallow, you can try to color it to match surrounding area. What you use depends on what kind of wood the furniture is made of.

On walnut furniture, try rubbing the meat of a walnut or Brazil nut or butternut (available at nut shops or candy stores) into the scratch. Follow by waxing the piece, and buffing.

If the piece is red mahogany, ordinary iodine sometimes colors it properly. Apply it to the scratch with a Q-Tip or, preferably, a number 0 artist's brush. Be careful not to drip the iodine on any surrounding surface. When the iodine is dry, wax and buff the piece.

For brown or cherry mahogany, iodine that has turned dark with age sometimes works. For maple, dilute the iodine about 50% with denatured alcohol.

Even shoe polish can be used to hide minor scratches. You can use a brown shade for walnut, a cordovan shade for mahogany, a tan shade for light finishes, and black

for black lacquered (very shiny) wood. Apply the polish
with a Q-Tip or with a toothpick that has a little cotton
wrapped around the end. If the color is too dark for the
wood (or too light), you can remove it with naphtha,
available at paint stores. Shoe polish is only good if the
finish is shiny, because when you wax and buff, the polish will shine.

Commercial liquid colorings are also available. These
come in little bottles in practically every wood shade, and
with little applicators. Get a good mental picture of the
color of the piece of furniture, then go down to your local paint store and have a look.

With liquid colorings, by the way, be they homemade
or commercial preparations, try them out first on an inconspicuous portion of the furniture. This test will tell
you better than anything how close a match the coloring
is.

Major scratches, or gouges, require filling to be effec-
tively concealed. As with minor ones, you have more
than one method at your disposal.

The simplest way—the least permanent, too—is with
wax sticks. These look like crayons and come in a wide
variety of colors to match wood tones.

First, clean out the scratch with a razor. Wipe with
naphtha. Rub the stick along the scratch, filling it and
working it level with a finger. Wipe with a soft cloth and
the job's done.

If the piece of furniture gets hard use, this type of repair is not likely to last terribly long. A more permanent
method—indeed, it's the one the pros use—is to use stick
shellac.

Stick shellacs are available in a great many different

colors to match various woods. Well-stocked paint stores carry them.

To use the shellac, heat a flexible knife, such as an artist's palette knife, a loose hacksaw blade, or a thin table knife. For heat, the best thing is an alcohol lamp (a cheap one costs $2 or so at hardware stores), because it doesn't produce soot—soot mixing with shellac will discolor it. You can also use a soldering iron, or any flame source. But if you use an open flame, quickly wipe the tool off to remove soot before applying the tool to the shellac.

Apply the heated tool to the shellac stick. Let shellac

Professionals use stick shellac to fill deep scratches. First, heat the shellac stick of the appropriate color and let it drip into the scratch. Slightly overfill.

drip into the scratch, or wipe it in with the tool. (The scratch, by the way, should be clean—scrape out with a razor blade and wipe clean with naphtha). Slightly overfill the scratch, let it dry, then shave it down level with

When dry, gently scrape off the excess with a razor blade. Then polish the patch with rottenstone and oil until it blends with the surrounding surface.

Another way to fill minor scratches is with padding lacquer, a special
kind of lacquer and blending stain, which is made in a variety of
wood colors. Just ball up a rag, apply lacquer and stain of the appropriate color, and rub it on the scratch.

the surrounding surface by scraping it with a single-edge razor blade held perpendicular to the surface. Or you can use a little piece of 6/0 grade sandpaper to sand it level. In any case, make sure you confine your shaving efforts to the shellac itself—try not to disturb the surrounding finish. Finally, polish with rottenstone (an inexpensive abrasive powder available at paint stores) and a little linseed oil. The more you polish, the shinier the patch will get. Polish until the patch matches the surrounding area as closely as possible.

Ink Stains

It's almost a waste of time to write about removing ink, because it's often impossible. The only answer is to completely refinish the piece of furniture.

If ink does spill, immediately blot up as much of it as you can with a blotter, paper towel, or bathroom tissue. Then pat the stain with a damp cloth. *Don't rub.* Keep turning the cloth so you're constantly blotting with a clean section. If all the ink doesn't come off, try rottenstone and oil, as explained under "White Marks."

Stains on Marble and Tile-Top Tables

These two materials also require instant attention if something is spilled on them. A spillage can really seep into marble or tile, and if there's grout—the stuff between tiles—it will be especially difficult to clean.

If you know what the stain is from, removal is very simple. For coffee, tea, fruit juice, and food stains, cold water and Spic and Span usually works. If it doesn't, use laundry bleach.

Spic and Span and cold water works on blood stains, too; these can also be bleached out with hydrogen perox-

ide. For ink stains, use laundry bleach or peroxide.
Grease spots yield to a mixture of one part sal soda to
nine parts water.

When you don't know what the stain is from, try a
variety of things until one works.

First, try Spic and Span and cold water. No luck? Try
turpentine or white vinegar. If these don't do it, graduate
to laundry bleach, trying to bleach out the stain. If this
doesn't make it, use 20 volume hydrogen peroxide or ammonia. Never use bleach and ammonia together. The
two combine to form a chemical with vapors that can lit-
erally kill.

When using any of the above cleaners, just wipe it on
and give it half an hour to do its work. Then clean the
area thoroughly with hot water and dry immediately
with a cloth. To protect your hands when using the
cleaner, wear rubber gloves.

If none of the cleaners works, try rubbing the stains
away with some sort of abrasive. On marble or tile, try a
mild treatment first, rubbing with fine-grade steel wool
and a scouring powder such as Comet (cold water). If
this doesn't do it, rub with fine-grade sandpaper and Spic
and Span—but not on glazed (shiny) tile. It can scratch
the finish.

Sticking Paper

Sometimes, if you put a hot object on paper on a
wooden piece of furniture, the paper will stick. Damp
newspaper will also stick. To remove either, wipe ordinary olive oil on the paper. Give it a chance to soak
through—a half hour—then rub off the paper and any
stain left with a clean cloth.

Newsprint or other paper that sticks can be removed with cooking oil. Wipe oil on the paper, give it time to soak in, then rub off with a clean cloth.

Burns

Some furniture blemishes, as you've seen, are removed in strange ways. But nothing compares with the way you handle a slight burn—with cigarette or cigar ash.

Actually, there's method behind the apparent madness. The ashes act like an abrasive and scour away the charred portion.

So, when you have a slight burn, dampen your finger and rub ashes over the burned area. When all the blackening is removed, wipe clean and apply a touch of wax.

If a burn is particularly deep, you use a more conventional method. First, remove as much of the charred area as you can by scraping it off with a knife or single-edge razor blade held perpendicular to the surface. Try not to scratch the surrounding area. Follow the scraping by wiping the area clean with a cotton swab dipped in naphtha, available at hardware stores. Smooth by rubbing

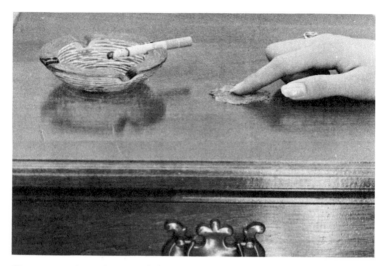

Cigarette or cigar ashes are mild abrasives that can be used to remove blackening from burns. Dampen a finger and rub ashes on the blackening until it disappears.

with extra-fine sandpaper (at hardware stores) and complete the face-lift by following the same method used to handle deep scratches.

Dents

By a dent, we mean a small area of the wood that has been compressed rather than actually gouged or cut.

The job here is to steam the wood so it swells up back into shape. This can take a while, but is does work.

First, use a wet cotton swab and some Soilax to remove wax and polish from the dent. Lay several thicknesses of cheesecloth or a plain folded cloth on the dent. Place a metal bottle cap, top down, on the cloth and directly over the dent. Press a hot iron on the bottle cap. This concentrates the steam. Keep the iron on the cap only a few seconds at a time, to avoid scorching the wood.

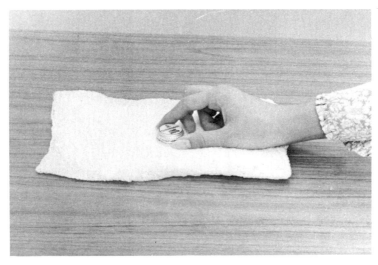

A dent in wood is handled by swelling the wood in the dent back into shape. Clean the area, then place a damp cloth on the area and put a bottle cap precisely over the dent.

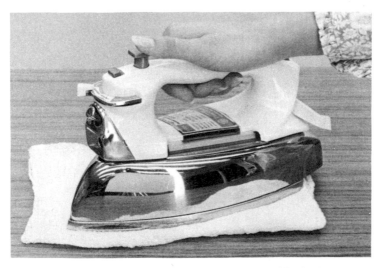

Apply a hot iron on the bottle cap. Steam is concentrated in the dent.

White Marks

There are two kinds of white marks that you may have to deal with: the white rings left by glasses containing water, alcohol, or what-have-you and the blotchy, cloudy patterns left by hot objects. You can follow the same removal procedure for both.

First, gently rub the mark with a dampened finger and cigar or cigarette ash; ordinary toothpaste can also be used. Follow the grain of the wood as you rub, and wipe clean when the stain disappears.

If the mark doesn't go away, it means that you need something more abrasive than ashes—namely, rottenstone.

Shake a little rottenstone into one saucer and pour a little cooking oil or linseed oil into another. Fold a small

White marks that are stubborn are removed with rottenstone and cooking oil. Place oil in one saucer, rottenstone in another. Dip a pad or cloth in oil, then rottenstone, and then rub the mark.

Whenever any rubbing is required, always polish with the grain, as shown.

Wax is removed with ice. Ice makes wax hard so you can chip it off.

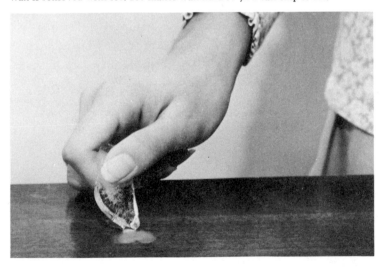

piece of felt or flannel cloth into a small pad. Dip the
pad in the oil, then in the rottenstone. Rub the blemish,
again following the wood grain. Use light pressure. If the
finish comes off in the process of removing the mark,
you can touch up later, applying a dab of the appropriate
finish with a small brush.

Candle Wax

Wax is easier to remove if you harden it first. To do
this, hold an ice cube against it for half a minute. Wipe
away the melted water, then use a dull knife (such as a
butter knife) to pick off as much wax as you can without
touching the wood. Then, very gently, scrape away the
portion that is sticking to the furniture. When all the wax
is gone, rub the area briskly with furniture wax and wipe
dry with a clean cloth.

Milk Stains

Milk, ice cream, or anything containing milk can
leave a bad blemish on furniture, because the lactic acid
in them eats right through the finish. At any rate, immediately wipe as much of it away as possible, and clean off
as much of the remaining stain as you can with furniture
wax. Then follow with the removal method given for
"White Marks."

Damaged Veneer

Veneer is the beautiful wood skin on wood furniture. A number of things can go wrong with it, all repair-
able.

A common problem is that it becomes loose—separ-
ates from the piece of furniture proper.

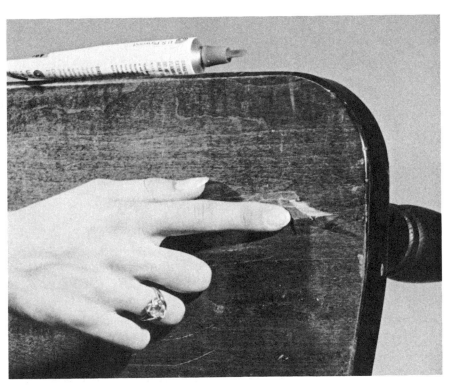

Loose or blistered veneer, such as shown here, can be repaired fairly
easily. See text for details.

If this happens, simply glue the veneer back in place
with white glue. First, though, clean out all old, hardened
glue and any food particles or other soil that may have
worked under it. Since veneer invariably loosens at the
edges of a piece, this shouldn't be a problem. Just take a
nail file, a knife, or some other thin-bladed instrument,
and scrape and blow the old glue and soil out. If you
don't do this, the new glue may not be able to hold the
veneer properly.

When the area under the veneer is clean, use a sliver
of wood or a toothpick to spread new glue in place. Press
the veneer in place, then pile heavy objects—a handful of
books will do—on the veneer until the glue has dried
thoroughly. As you press the veneer down, some glue
will likely squeeze out. Clean this off immediately with
a rag. If a little remains, no sweat—white glue dries clear.

Another problem with veneer is a blister, or bubble.
Sometimes the bubble is split; other times it's not. If it's
split, poke into the opening with a damp Q-Tip to clean
it out as well as you can. If there's no split, make a small
incision along the length of the blister with a single-edge
razor blade.

Smear white glue inside (under) the raised veneer.
Place a piece of wax paper over the veneer, then place
very heavy books or some other weight on it to force it
down in position. If you can see that the veneer will not
be forced flat by the weight, first apply a damp rag to it
until it becomes pliable enough to do so.

When the glue has dried (overnight is more than
enough), pick and sand away the wax paper, using medium-grade sandpaper. Then wax and buff the entire surface.

Sometimes veneer on the edge of a piece of furniture chips off. If you're lucky, you may recover the broken piece. Just glue it back in place, using the wax paper on top of which you've piled books or other weights.

It is likely, however, that you won't have the broken-off piece. If this is the case, you have to make a patch with new veneer.

New veneer may be obtained from old pieces at junk-yard dealers or from another piece of furniture where it won't show. Or, if the patch needed is very large, you can buy a whole sheet of new veneer at a lumberyard. Constantine's, Bronx, N.Y., also sells veneer samples that can be used for patching.

At any rate, the key is to get veneer that matches the color and grain of the wood in the existing furniture as closely as possible, so that it blends in unobtrusively.

Cut a patch big enough to cover the spot where the veneer is missing. The patch may be cut in a rectangle, a triangle, or any other shape with straight lines.

Place the patch over the spot where veneer is missing and, using a steel ruler or other hard straightedge and a razor blade, carefully cut around the edges of the patch and through one layer of veneer. Then simply remove the cutout material and glue the patch in place as described.

3

Sick Furniture

Besides scratches, stains, and the like, wooden furniture is subject to a variety of maladies that have to do with the structure of the particular piece. Following are some of the things that can go wrong and how to cure them.

Loose Chair Rung

All parts of chairs are susceptible to loosening, but it seems especially true of rungs. The problem usually occurs in the winter. The low humidity (little moisture in the air), combined with house heat, evaporates the moisture in wood fibers, and the wood shrinks. In the case of rungs, which are usually secured in their sockets with glue, the ends shrink and vibrations from using the chair ultimately breaks the glue seal. Hence, a loose rung.

It's always easier to fix the rung if you can remove its end from the socket. Sometimes there's enough "play" —looseness—to do this. But don't try and remove it if it's in pretty tight. In the process you could loosen other parts.

If you can get the rung out, follow this procedure. Using a small knife, scrape away all old glue—from the rung and inside the socket—down to clean, bare wood. Apply a coat of white glue to the rung and the socket; a cotton swab is handy here. White glue is available at hardware stores. Two brands are Elmer's and U.S. Plywood's White Glue. A small bottle costs 50¢ or so.

Immediately after applying the glue, stick the rung back into its socket. Make a cord tourniquet, as shown in the photo. Wrap a length of clothesline around the chair. Tie a knot, then slip a stick under the cord and turn the stick so the cord winds up and acts like a tourniquet, pulling the rung and the part it fits into tightly together. Then tie or position the stick on the chair so the cord doesn't unwind. Check around the socket for forced-out glue and wipe it off with a rag. Let the glue dry overnight, then take the cord off. That's it.

If there was a real gap around the rung—say an eighth of an inch—glue alone probably won't work. So do this. Clean off all old glue as before. Apply fresh white glue to the rung end, then tightly wind string around it. Coat the socket with glue, then force the end into place. Make a cord tourniquet as before and then, with a single-edge razor blade, trim off any string sticking out of the socket. Let dry.

Of course, it is highly likely that you won't be able to get the rung out without making other chair parts loose. If you can't, no sweat. There is a liquid product

A loose chair part can be fixed by injecting a product like Devcon Grip-Wood into the joint. This swells the wood, making for tighter fit, and reglues at the same time.

Clamp the parts tightly together until the product dries. A home-made cord tourniquet can be made by wrapping a cord around the chair, inserting a stick through the cord, and then turning stick round and round until the cord winds up and pulls the parts together. The end of the stick can be hooked in some part of the chair so the cord doesn't unwind. Wood blocks under the cord keep it from rubbing against the chair.

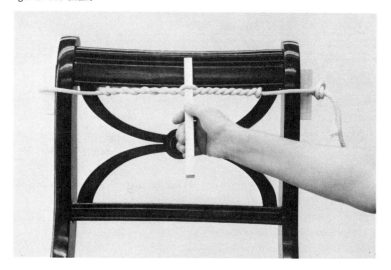

called Devcon Grip-Wood (at hardware stores for about
$1.75), that makes the repair easy. It comes with syringe-
like applicator on it that lets you inject the product into
the space around the rung end. Inside, the product will
make the wood swell up and will act as an adhesive at
the same time. That's all there is to it. However, for best
results, position the chair so gravity lets the liquid flow
down into the socket. Incidentally, you can buy Grip-
Wood without the special applicator for around 75¢.

Sticking Drawer

Did you ever notice that drawers on dressers, vanities,
and the like usually stick during the summer or in damp
weather? The reason is that humidity is high and moisture gets into the wood and swells the fibers—in effect,
the drawer becomes a wee bit too big for the compartment it fits into.

Usually, a little lubrication is all that's needed. Just
apply candle wax, paraffin, or a silicon spray (at hardware stores) to the parts of the drawer that are binding.
You can usually tell these parts because they'll have a
dark, almost polished look—from rubbing. At any rate, if
the drawer is simply the box type, first clear away all
dust and then lubricate the sides and bottom. If it's the
kind that has thin wood strips on the sides that ride in
grooves, lubricate the strips; if it has a wood strip in the
center on the bottom, lubricate it and the sides. In other
words, lubricate wherever wood contacts wood.

If the drawer is so badly stuck that you can't remove
it for lubricating, you'll have to shrink the wood first.

You do this with heat. One good thing to use is a so-
called drop light—a bulb enclosed in a little wire cage;

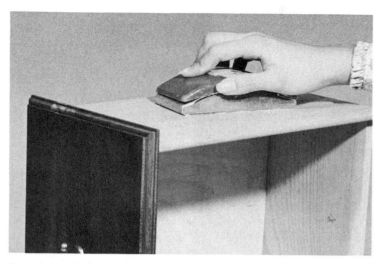

Some drawers have to be sanded a little to make them slide better. You can wrap sandpaper around a little wooden block or use the inexpensive tool shown above—or simply fold the paper.

the bulb itself is on an extension cord (the cost of this drop light is around $1.50). Just place the bulb inside the drawer for an hour or two. You could also use a portable hair dryer, directing heat in the drawer, a 60-watt light bulb in an ordinary lamp—in fact any source of heat. But check after an hour to see how the drawer is sliding—you don't want to dry everything out too much.

If you can't get the drawer open far enough to blow the heat in or get the bulb in, remove the drawer above or below it and put the bulb in either compartment, or blow the heat from there.

If you can't budge the drawer, work carefully with a screwdriver to pry it out. But this shouldn't be required. When you get the drawer out, lubricate it as described earlier.

When lubrication doesn't make the drawer slide eas-

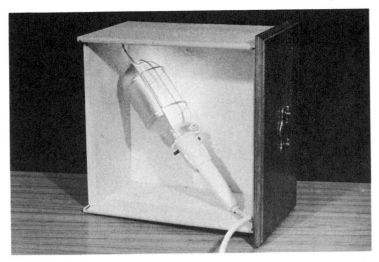

If you can't get a drawer out, moisture may be the reason—it swells wood. To shrink it, place a light such as shown above in the drawer to dry it out.

ily, you can use sandpaper to slim it down a smidgeon at critical points. First clean off the lubrication with turpentine or Spic and Span on a damp rag. Wrap a medium-grade piece of sandpaper (at hardware stores) around a small block of wood you can hold in your hand. Sand, stopping and checking frequently to see how the drawer is sliding; you don't want to take off too much wood.

If you push a drawer in and it sticks at the last inch or so, it probably means that the bottom of each side is worn down, whereas the front is not. To correct this, remove the drawer and press in a line of thumbtacks along the paths where each edge rides. The tacks raise the drawer and let it slide easily, as if it were on railroad tracks. Of course, you'll have to raise or lower the tacks to get it sliding just the way it should.

Another possible cause of a sticking drawer is that

the piece of furniture is resting on an uneven floor. When this happens, one side of the dresser, or vanity, or whatever may sag so that the compartment that the drawer goes in becomes misaligned.

You can tell this if there are uneven amounts of space around the drawer. If this is the case, stick pieces of cardboard or wood slivers under the piece of furniture to raise it level so the drawer (or drawers) do not rub against the compartment.

Of course, a drawer can stick simply because some object inside the drawer is jammed up in the compartment. You can solve this easily if there is no partition above the drawer. Just take out the drawer above it and remove the object. Otherwise, pull the drawer out as far as you can and pick the items out one by one. Or stick a table knife between the closed drawer and the framework and poke the object free.

Drawer Closes Crooked

Another drawer problem occurs when you push in the drawer and one side goes in further than the other. This is because a piece of wood in the back of the compartment is loose or gone and does not stop the drawer as it's supposed to.

To cure this, forget the compartment and work on the drawer. As shown in the photo, cut (with a saw) a piece of wood as high as the back of the drawer and as thick as the extra distance it travels in. To find the latter dimension, push the drawer in and measure (with a ruler rather than tape measure) from the face of the drawer on the side that goes in too far, to the front of the compartment. Glue this little block of wood onto the back of the side that goes in too far. Let dry.

If a drawer closes crooked, glue a piece of wood on the side that goes in too far. The wood should be the thickness of the extra distance the drawer travels in.

Loose Countertop Material

I'm talking here about plastic laminate, the hard sheeting that is used to cover kitchen and other countertops. Occasionally it comes loose and has to be fastened again.

The refastening is done with contact cement, a glue that sticks things together on contact. Normally, when using contact cement, you apply a coat of it to one surface (the bottom of the laminate) and a coat to the surface it rests on (the top of the cabinet). Then you wait an hour or so, until the cement is dry and press the surfaces together. They stick on contact.

However, loose plastic laminate usually isn't loose enough so you can apply a coat of cement to each surface. So, to make the repair, lift the laminate up as far as you can without cracking it. Load a little paint brush (around 29¢) with a big glob of the cement and shove it in under the laminate. Press the laminate down as far as you can and *immediately* lift it up again. Keep the laminate propped up with a fork for an hour or so—until the cement's dry—and then take out the fork and press the laminate down against the surface, banging on it with your fist to get a good bond. That's it.

Until recently, contact cement was only available in a flammable form with harmful vapors. Now, however, you can get a kind that is nonflammable and safe in every way. One brand is Weldwood's Home Safe Contact Cement. A pint, all you need for the job, is listed at $1.13 in a recent catalog.

When refastening loose plastic laminate, prop it up with a fork until the contact cement is dry.

Table Wobbles

When a kitchen, dining-room or other type of table wobbles or shakes without the slightest provocation, you have to check out a variety of things to see what's causing the problem.

One common cause is that a leg is loose. On most tables there is a bolt with a nut—it looks like a square donut—on each of the legs where it joins the table. When a nut is loose, the bolt will be—and so will the leg.

Just check the nuts. If there's looseness in one, use a wrench or a pair of pliers to tighten it up by turning clockwise.

Some tables have legs fastened on with screws or wingnuts. The former are fair game for a screwdriver, the latter can be tightened with your fingers. If you see another type of fastener, don't worry: Tighten as needed.

Another reason for a wobbly table is that not all the legs are resting squarely on the floor because it's uneven—not perfectly flat. So every time weight is put on the table on the not-resting-leg side, down goes the table top ... wobble, wobble.

For this, try moving the table to a new position so all legs touch the floor.

If this doesn't work it means that a leg is too short. For this just place a piece of cardboard or a sliver of wood under the offending leg so it has nowhere to dip—there's no space under it. To solve the problem, cut out a piece of cardboard, wood or other fairly solid material and glue it to the leg bottom with white glue.

No matter the repair, you'll find it easier to work

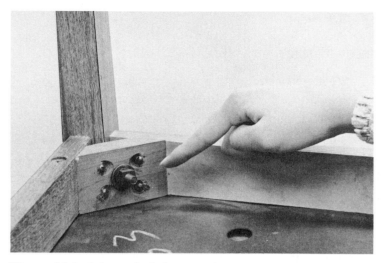

When a table leg is loose, check the nut under the table at each corner. If a nut is loose, this could cause problems. Tighten with a wrench or a pair of pliers.

with the table turned over. But if it's too heavy for this, no sweat. If a loose leg is the problem, just crawl under the table to make the repair. If you want to glue material to a short leg, just coat the shim (as the pros say) with glue, lift the table a little, and put it in place.

Loose Casters

Loose furniture casters make it difficult, and sometimes impossible, to roll a piece of furniture around. Actually, it's not the caster that's loose but the metal socket it fits into. This socket is attached to the furniture by little metal teeth that bite into and grip the wood—it's the teeth that lose their grip.

For the repair, you need four things: a hammer, a screwdriver, a little petroleum jelly, and steel glue, an adhesive that will stick steel to wood. A good brand is Devcon's Plastic Steel. A two-ounce kit (it comes in two tubes you mix together before using) costs about a dollar.

First, carefully pry off the socket by inserting a screwdriver under the teeth and lifting. When it's off, coat the inside of the socket—the part the caster fits into—with petroleum jelly. Later, if glue oozes in there, the caster won't be accidentally bonded in place.

Mix the Plastic Steel, following label directions; then coat the outside of the socket with the glue. Insert the socket into the leg, then use the hammer, gently but firmly, to tap it back into place so the teeth bite into the wood. Let dry, then stick the caster back in place.

If a caster is loose, it usually means that the socket that fits into the leg is loose. Take out the caster, then carefully pry out the socket with a screwdriver.

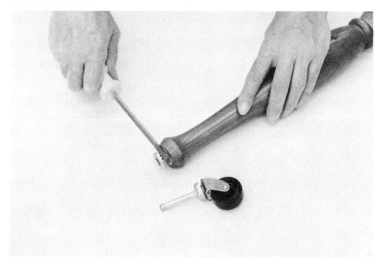

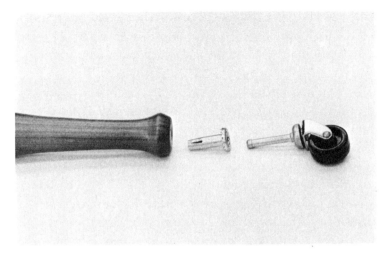

This is how parts look in proper relation to one another.

Squeeze some steel glue on the socket, then press it into the hole in the leg. Also apply some petroleum jelly inside the metal socket. Glue that oozes inside won't make the caster stick permanently.

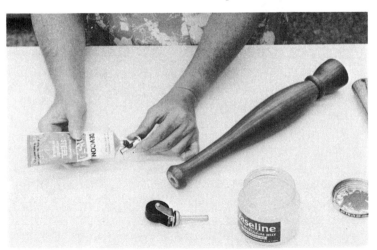

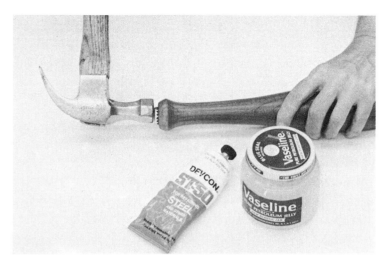

With the socket in the leg, gently hammer it so the prongs on the socket bite into the wood. That's it.

Loose Drawer Knob

You can hardly call this a repair, it's so simple.

Pull out the drawer and hold the knob stationary with one hand. Using a nail file, tighten the screw inside that holds the knob on. That's it.

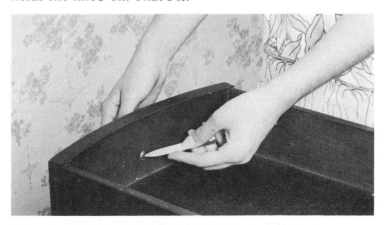

A loose knob on a drawer is easily fixed. Hold the knob tight and tighten the screw with nail file.

4

Electrical Problems

The repairs least attempted by do-it-yourselfers are electrical ones. The reason is simple. Fear. Fear of a shocking experience or possibly burning the house down.

Actually, many electrical repairs should be left to the "pro." Indeed, all communities prohibit anyone but the professional from making certain ones.

Happily, though, there are some that can be made without approval and with no hazard whatsoever. And these are commonly the ones that need to be done. Let's take a look at them.

Plug Keeps Coming Out of Socket

Plugs from appliances and lamps often fall out of wall receptacles or outlets. The reason is usually that the plug prongs are bent or misshapen and can't get a grip. Or the receptacle may be a little worn. To solve the problem, simply bend the prongs outward with your fingers a little.

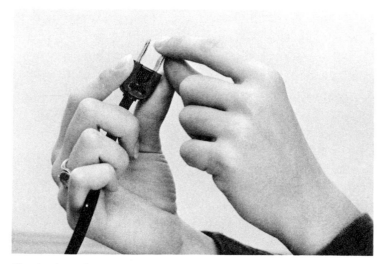

If a plug keeps falling out of the wall, spread the prongs apart a little with your fingers.

Stick the plug in the receptacle. Gently pull on it. Does it stick? No? Bend the prongs out a little further.

Broken Plug

When a plug is corroded, or cracked, or damaged some other way, it's a good idea to replace it. Indeed, it may be the reason why a lamp or small appliance doesn't work, and should be suspected immediately.

There are two kinds of plugs. One is "sealed," so-called because the ends of the electrical wires are buried inside it. There's no way to get at the wires that go into it without cutting open and ruining the plug. The other kind is "open construction," so-called because it has a removable fiber disc that slips over the plug prongs and snaps into place. This disc can be removed, revealing the bare wire ends of the electrical cord.

Whatever type you have now, buy an "open-construction" type replacement. Just show the old kind to your hardware store dealer and get a new one like it, but making sure it's the open-construction kind. Plugs come in various colors to match electrical cords and cost about 30¢ or 40¢.

To make the replacement, first cut off the old plug with a pair of scissors. Just snip off the plug and a little of the cord. If the cord is actually two molded sections, split it in half lengthwise about two inches by pulling it apart with your fingers. If the cord has a cloth covering, cut this off to a length of two inches to expose the rubber-covered groups of wires (or single wires). With a razor blade, carefully slice off about three quarters of an inch of rubber from each section, exposing two separate groups of hair-thin bare wires. With your fingers, smooth the sets of wires out, as you would before braiding hair.

Snap out the fiber disc with a screwdriver. Slip the two inches of rubber and wires through the hole in the plug. Tie an "underwriter's knot" as shown in the sketch, loosen the screw, then wind one group of wires under one screw, tighten the screw, and do the same for the other group of wires. Push the wires down between the prongs (make sure the separate groups of wires don't touch) and snap in the fiber disc with your fingers. That's it.

Frayed Cord

Cloth covering on electrical cords is often subject to fraying, usually close to the plug.

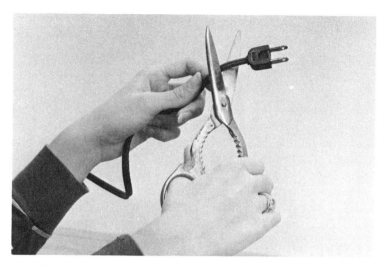

To replace a bad plug, first cut off the bad one with shears or a razor blade.

Pull the cord apart so it splits in two for a distance of two inches or so. Then trim the rubber off the wire with a sharp knife or razor, exposing three quarters of an inch of bare wire on each section.

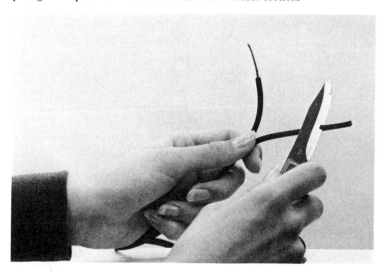

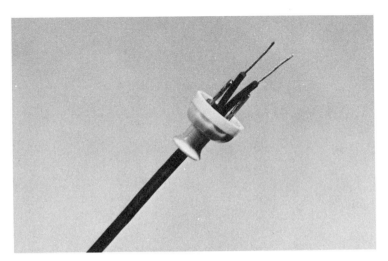

Thread the prepared wires through the hole in the new socket. Use an open-construction type.

Tie a so-called underwriter's knot in the cord. This will prevent the cord from slipping back through the hole in the plug.

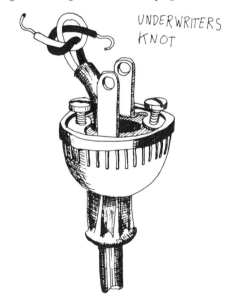

UNDERWRITERS
KNOT

Wrap each wire around each prong as shown, then wind the exposed part of each under each of the little screws. It doesn't matter which wire goes to which screw. Tighten the screws. Slip the fiber disc over prongs and snap it in place.

To repair this, simply cut the cord off at the point where the frayed section begins. Take off the fiber disc from the plug, loosen the screws holding the wires, and pull out the piece of cord. Discard it, then attach the cord wires to the plug as if you were replacing the plug. (Described under "Broken Plug.")

Appliances Don't Work

There are many reasons why refrigerators, freezers, washing machines, and other big appliances go "on the blink." There are a few things you can try before calling the repairman.

First, though it may sound obvious, check to see if the appliance is plugged in. Check not only the plug that goes into the wall socket, but the plug that plugs into the appliance itself. Many a repairman has charged $15 or $20 for a service call that consisted of only this.

If both plugs are in, examine the plug that goes into the wall. Does it look in good shape? It does? Then open it up—pry off the fiber disc—and check to see if the wires are tightly secured to the two little screws. If one is loose, wind it around under the screw head and tighten the screw. That will solve the problem. If the plug isn't in good shape, replace it as described under "Broken Plug."

If the wall plug is okay, check the appliance plug.

These plugs look like little flat boxes, a lot different from open-construction or sealed plugs, but they are really alike—and the repair is almost the same.

To check the appliance plug, first pull the wall plug out of the socket. This eliminates any electrical hazard.

Split the plug into halves by either unscrewing little screws in it or, on some, simply snapping it apart. Inside, you'll see two wires, each attached to a little screw, just

This kind of appliance plug comes apart easily by taking the small screws out, then snapping the sections apart. The wires are attached to clips inside.

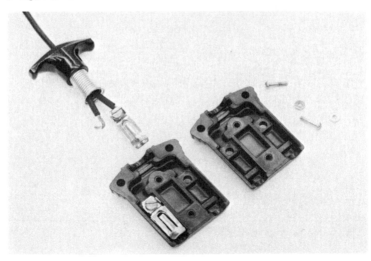

as in a regular plug. If either is loose, resecure it under its little screws (as you did with the open-construction plug) and the problem should be solved.

Even though they may not yet have interfered with the working of an appliance, a frayed cord or broken plug body should be remedied immediately. For a frayed cord, first open up the plug. Each screw is attached to a little metal clip. Cut the plug off, including the frayed portion of the cord. Loosen the screws and snap out the clips. Draw the cord out and discard.

Prepare the ends of the cord as for a regular broken plug, stripping off three quarters of an inch of rubber from each group of wires. Slip the cord through the spring wire guard attached to the plug, then through the hole in the plug. Also, as before, draw two inches of it through the plug hole. Tie an underwriter's knot in the wires, as shown in the sketch. Tie each wire to a screw and snap the clips back in. Then snap the plug halves back together.

Broken Lamp

If a lamp flickers or doesn't go on, it could be a bad bulb.

If a new bulb doesn't solve the problem, check the wall plug: Are the prongs getting a good grip in the wall? How about the plug itself? Are the wires in it securely attached under the little screws? Is the plug broken? Handle any problem as previously described.

If the wall plug is okay, the trouble is inside the lamp.

Pull the plug out of the wall and set the lamp on a table where you have a good working light.

Take out the bulb, then unscrew the cap on the very

top of the lamp; take off the shade and then the harp, the wire section around the bulb.

The shiny metal part that the bulb screws into is called the shell. On it, you'll see imprinted the word PRESS. Push on the word PRESS with your thumb, at the same time twisting the shell upward very hard. It will slip off. Inside the shell is a fiber liner shaped just like it. It may come off with the shell. If it doesn't, lift it off (this is easy to do).

To take a lamp apart, remove the shade and the harp (the metal wire around the bulb). Then look for word PRESS on the metal shell.

Put your thumb on the word PRESS. Press hard and twist the shell upwards. When it's loose, lift it off. Lift off the fiber shell under the metal shell.

Inside you'll see two wires, each attached to a little screw, as in a plug. If either is loose, tighten it up. If they're broken, cut off the cord and prepare and attach new wires, just as with a broken plug. If the socket itself is damaged, simply loosen the screws and slip out the wires. Lift the socket off and get a replacement like it at your hardware store. As with a plug, tie the wires to the screws. Finally, put the lamp back together by reversing the procedure you used to take it apart. Sockets, by the way, cost about 75¢.

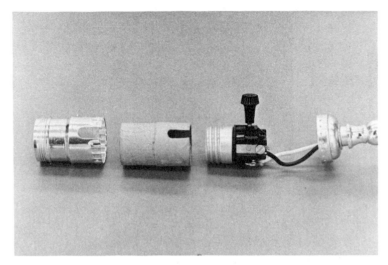

The disassembled lamp looks like this.

Check the wires that go to the little screws. Each wire should be in place with the screw tight over it. If not, the lamp will not work.

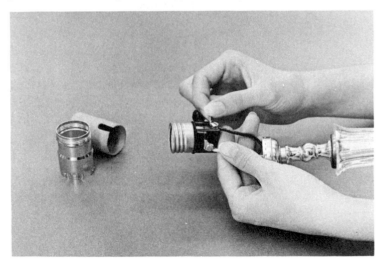

Flickering or Burnt-Out Fluorescent Tube

Like regular lamps, fluorescent tubes indicate something is wrong by flickering or simply not going on. A variety of simple things can cause problems.

If, when you flip on the light switch, the tube blinks repeatedly before it stays lit, that may mean that it's loose. Gently grasp it at the ends and turn it away from you to see if that seats it more securely; if it doesn't, turn it toward you to try to get it in tighter.

If it still flickers after tightening—or tightening wasn't needed—the problem may be caused by loose sockets that the ends of the tube fit into. The sockets are held on by screws on the outside ends of the metal housing. Try tightening them.

If the tube still flickers, probably a defective "starter" is causing the difficulty. This is a little barrel-shaped device that sits in a hole in the metal housing. To see it, you have to remove the tube.

Grasp the tube near the ends and turn it gently, first in one direction, then the other, until you hear a little blip; continue to turn that way until you hear another blip. Lift out the tube. When replacing it, reverse the process.

Most starters have the word REMOVE imprinted on the end, with a little arrow pointing left or right. First press the starter in as far as you can, then turn it in the direction of the arrow and lift out.

Take the starter down to your hardware store and get a replacement just like it (the cost is about 25¢). Install it by reversing the way you took it out. Other indi-

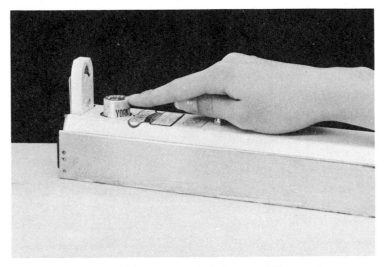

Fluorescent tubes can flicker because of a bad starter. When getting a new one, show the old one to the hardware dealer.

Sometimes the mountings that hold the tube become loose and the tube will flicker. Tightening the screw on each mounting usually solves the problem.

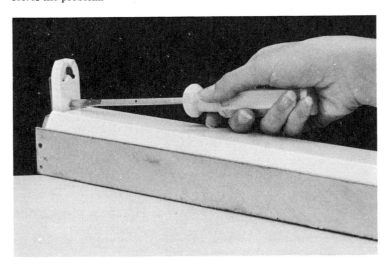

cations of a defective starter are when the ends of the tube glow brighter than the middle part, or when the light switch has to be flipped several times before the tube stays lit.

If all else fails, replace the tube. But a bad tube is unlikely, because they're designed to last hundreds of hours.

Lights Go Out or Appliances Stop Working Suddenly

Did you ever have the experience of working in the kitchen or elsewhere with a lot of appliances or other devices plugged in and when somebody turned on the TV or plugged in another appliance, everything went off?

The reason was that a fuse blew or, if you live in a fairly modern house, the so-called circuit breaker tripped.

The fuse, which serves the same purpose as the circuit breaker, is a safety device. It is part of your electrical wiring system, and when the wires are working too hard—because that extra thing was plugged in—the fuse blowing or the circuit breaker tripping stops everything. If the fuse or circuit breaker wasn't there, the wires could heat up and malfunction to the point of starting a fire.

First thing to do is to unplug the extra appliance. Then find the bad fuse or tripped circuit breaker. If you live in an apartment, you'll have four or more fuses and they'll likely be in a little metal box on a wall either in the kitchen or near it. If you live in a house, they'll probably be in the basement.

Open the little door on the box and look closely at the fuses. The fuses are little round things with tiny windows. The bad one will have a blackened window, or a little silver strip behind the window will be broken. Compare it to the other fuses and you'll immediately see the difference.

Stand on a dry board—never mix water and electricity!—and unscrew the fuse. Then take it down to your hardware store and get one just like it. It may say "15 amps" on it, or "20 amps." Anyway, your dealer will give you the right one. It'll cost about 15¢.

Circuit breakers will also be in a box on a wall. They look very much like ordinary light switches.

Look at them. See how all of them have the word ON showing. Except one. The tripped circuit breaker will say OFF. Then just flip it to ON. It accomplishes the same thing as putting in a new fuse.

To avoid the problem in the future, just don't plug that extra thing in. If you want to, you'll have to get new wiring installed. And this is the province of an electrician. Incidentally, if fuses blow or circuit breakers trip frequently without plugging in extra appliances, the wiring should be checked.

Iron Doesn't Work

When you turn on the iron and it doesn't work, it's likely that one of the wires inside the iron is loose. To find out, use a little screwdriver and remove the plate where the cord disappears into the iron, in back. Inside, you'll see that the cord splits into two wires, and that each wire has a little metal thing on the end, called a grommet, and is attached to a little screw. That is, only one grommet will be on, the other will be loose—that's

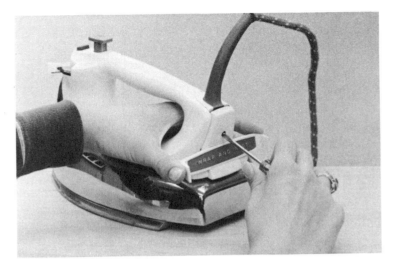

To take an iron apart, use a tiny screwdriver (one for sewing machine works well) and unscrew one or two screws that hold the back plate on.

This exposes the screws inside. Each wire should be wound around a screw and the screw should be turned down tightly over the wire.

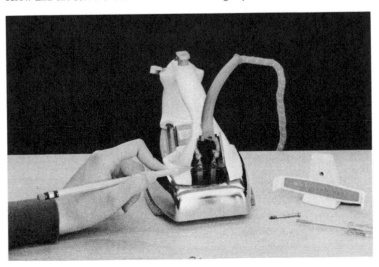

the problem. So, simply slip the grommet back onto the screw shaft where it belongs and tighten the screw on it.

Many times iron cords become frayed and require replacement. So, take the plate off in the back of the iron, loosen the screws holding the grommets on and take the cord to a hardware store or electrical supplies dealer and get one just like it. Then slip the grommets on the screws, tighten the screws and replace the plate.

5

Door Troubles

Sticking Door

If a regular door sticks when you try to close it, chances are that the top hinge is loose—the door sags and its bottom rubs against the floor—you'll probably see scuff marks on the floor.

A loose hinge means loose screws. Tighten them up and the problem's solved.

First, open the door all the way and stick as many thin books as you can under the outer door edge. This keeps it steady while you work and stops the door from pulling on the screws as you try to tighten them.

Tighten all the screws you can see—even the ones that don't look loose—as tight as you can. (You turn the screws to the right.) This will include the screws that go through the hinge into the door and those that go into the door opening framework (technically known as the jamb). Take away the books and try the door. It should

If a regular door sticks, it usually means the upper hinge is loose.
Tighten the screws.

work. If it still sticks, it's a job for a carpenter or handyman to fix.

Sometimes you won't be able to tighten the screws well because the screw holes on the wall framework are too chewed up—there isn't enough solid wood for the screws to bite into. Holes in the door itself usually stay good.

To handle this problem, first wedge up the door with thin books (or one fairly thick book). Take out all the screws in the hinge and turn back the hinge leaf. Pack Plastic Wood (a can is available at hardware stores for about 60¢) into the bad holes. (You'll know which ones these are because you'll never quite succeed in tightening up the screws in them. The screws will just keep turning, even though the heads are all the way in; if you look closely you will also see how chewed up they are.) Pack the Plastic Wood into each hole with a finger, poking at it with the tip of a screwdriver to eliminate air pockets. Fill each hole all the way and smooth it off with your finger. Let the Plastic Wood dry according to label directions.

Finally, drive in new screws where needed, the same kind as were used before but a half-inch longer. (Show the old screws to your hardware store dealer.) Take your time and drive the screws all the way in. The combination of Plastic Wood and the extra length of the screws—enabling them to bite into new wood—should solve the problem once and for all.

If you wish, you can pack white-glue-coated wooden match sticks (without the heads) into the screwholes. This serves the same purpose as the Plastic Wood.

If the screwholes are worn, pack them with Plastic Wood or
matchsticks and glue.

Loose Doorknob

Doorknobs have an annoying way of coming loose, making it difficult and sometimes impossible to open doors.

To remedy the condition, first look for a little screw on the neck (the narrow part) of the doorknob. Using a screwdriver, turn the little screw two or three full turns to the left to loosen it. Have someone hold the knob on the other side of the door so it can't move (or hold it yourself) and turn the knob on your side all the way to the right, pushing it forward as you do, until the front of the neck contacts the plate on the door. This may require a little muscle.

When the neck is snug against the plate, turn the knob back and forth to see how it works. If it's too tight (the latch won't come out after going in), turn the knob to your left about a quarter turn to loosen it. Then tighten up the little screw. That's it.

Cabinet Door Won't Shut

Many cabinet doors have two parts: a prong-like affair on the door and the part on the shelf that the prong fits into when you close the door. When the door doesn't shut, it's because repeated door closings have knocked the shelf part (the catch) out of line and the prong isn't fitting into it.

To get the door to shut properly, all you have to do is reposition the shelf part. On close inspection, you'll see that it's held on by two screws that go through a slot (rather than a hole). Loosen each of the screws a half turn to the left so you can slide the catch forward. As

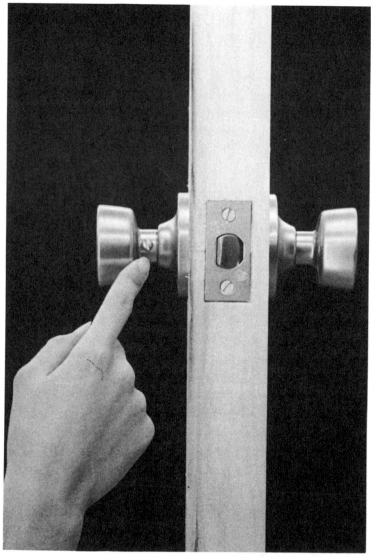

If a doorknob is loose, the little screw on the neck will be loose.

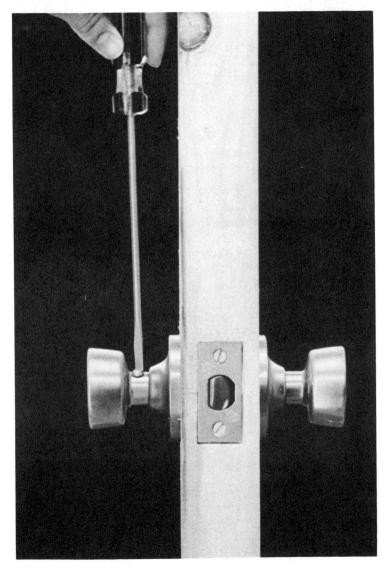

Turn the screw a few turns to the left to loosen it some more.

Turn the knob to the right (hold the other knob with your other
hand) until the neck contacts the plate on the door. Then tighten
the screw.

you do, straighten it out. Try the door. Does it stay closed? No? Then reposition the catch until it does. Then tighten up the screws. To prevent a recurrence, drive another little screw against the back of the slot.

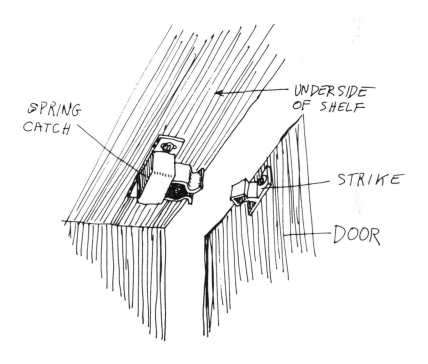

To make a cabinet door shut properly, loosen the screws holding the spring catch and reposition the catch so the strike on the door goes into it properly.

6

Window Troubles

The two main problems with windows are when they become stuck and when the glass breaks. Both problems are fairly easily cleared up.

Stuck Windows

If you can't open (or close) a wooden window, a likely reason is that dried paint has stuck it to the track it rides in.

To free the window, stick a knife in where the window meets the framework. Run the knife up and down—this may cut the dried paint. Another way: Take a hammer and tap all around the window frame, using a little wood block or a folded towel to protect the window finish. This vibrates the window and breaks the paint seal.

Once you get a window moving, open and close it 10 or 15 times. Then apply a liberal amount of lubrication in the track. You can use wax or a silicone spray; Sears sells an eight-ounce can of the latter for a little over a dollar.

Another reason for a wooden window to stick is that it's lopsided in its track. You pull up, or down, and the one side jams against the track.

The cure here is to get the window level before you attempt to move it. Pull along the bottom to get it level, then carefully keep it level every time you raise or lower it. Also lubricate the track. Repair involves taking the window down, and this is outside the scope of this book. It's a job for a professional.

If the window is stuck or sticking for no apparent reason, apply lubrication and try to get it moving.

Casement windows—the metal ones that open by turning a little crank handle—can also become stuck. Paint builds up on the bottom edge, or the hinge screws come loose, allowing the window to sag—and stick. The cure in the first case is to scrape off the paint from the bottom edge with a scraper or a butter knife. Tightening the screws will solve the second problem.

When sliding windows stick, it's usually because the lower tracks they slide in get clogged with soil. Brushing out the dirt should solve the problem. Follow this by spraying a silicone spray into the track.

Broken Windows

The hardest part of this job is cutting a new piece of glass to fit into the window frame. And you don't have to do it. You can get a piece cut to size free by a professional at the glass shop where you get the new glass. (See the Yellow Pages, under "Glass.") And you can get the glass cheaply. I recently bought a 14-by-20-inch piece of single-strength glass for $1.25.

We're talking here about replacing glass in a wooden frame window, either little panes or big ones. Replacing glass in an iron window is better left to a professional.

First, take out the broken glass. Wear heavy work gloves. Get a grip on a broken section and gently rock it back and forth until it comes out. Repeat for other broken sections. If the glass isn't broken enough to get a grip on it, gently tap it with a hammer until it is. Wear sunglasses to protect your eyes.

With the glass out, scrape away all the old putty from the window frame. Do a good job, going down to clean, bare wood. When the scraping is complete, brush out, or use a rag to wipe out all putty crumbs.

As you remove the putty, you'll notice little triangu-

The first step in replacing a broken window is removing the broken glass. Wear tough gloves that glass can't cut. Rock the pieces back and forth gently to remove them, pulling out at the same time.

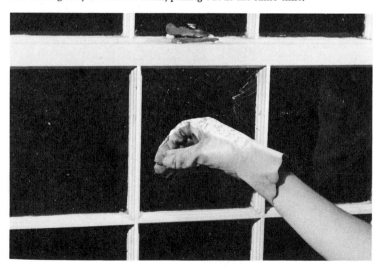

Using a putty knife, remove all old putty down to clean, bare wood. Use two hands on the putty knife, if necessary. Use pliers to pull out "points"—triangles of metal that hold the glass on.

lar pieces of metal sticking into the frame. These are called glazier's points, and their job is to hold the glass in place—it's not the putty that does this. Remove them with a pair of pliers or a screwdriver. Note the places they were removed from. You can mark them with a pencil or crayon.

When the frame is clean, apply a coat of exterior paint to it. The wood is likely to be dry and will suck in the paint rather than the juices of the new glazing compound you'll use.

Measure for the glass as shown in one of the accompanying photos—from edge to edge inside the frame, both horizontally and vertically. When you have the dimensions, subtract an eighth of an inch from each. For example, if your vertical measurement is 12 inches, subtract the eighth and you get 11-7/8 inches. Order the

Very carefully measure the window frame. This is the key to success. Measure the inside of the framework, both length and width.

glass in this size. The smaller glass gives you more space and allows the framework to expand and contract due to weather. To be sure you're measuring accurately, it's a good idea to do it three times at different points on the window.

If you're replacing glass in a little (multi-paned) window, order single-strength glass. For a large (single pane) window, order double-strength.

You'll also need a little can of glazing compound, which is the modern counterpart of putty. Glazing compound is more expensive than putty, but it's easier to work with and is more flexible—it doesn't dry out like putty. One brand is Red Devil; a can costs about 80¢.

First, mix the compound in the can with a narrow putty knife (it looks like a thin spatula). Scoop out a little on the end of your knife and apply a thin—cardboard

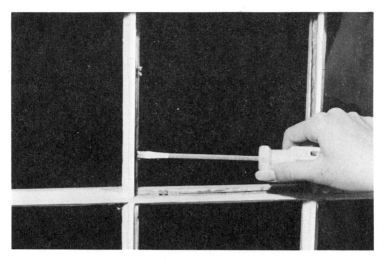

Using a putty knife, spread a very thin bed of glazing compound all round the inside of the framework where the glass will be. Then insert the glass, and force new points in right next to the glass with a screwdriver.

thin—layer of it all around the window frame wood where the glass will rest.

Place the new glass all the way inside the frame. Push the glazier's points into the frame near their original holes. Each point should go in about halfway. For pushing you can use the end of a chisel, a screwdriver, a putty knife, or a quarter. The best points to get are those with little raised sections that allow them to be pushed in easily (One brand: Zip Points). A box of fifty or so costs about a quarter.

Now apply the glazing compound to the window where it meets the frame. Do this by scooping out small globs of it, pressing them along on the frame in the approximate finish shape you want it to have; check the putty on other windows for this. When one frame side is done, smooth the compound out into final shape by drawing the putty knife along it as shown in the sketch.

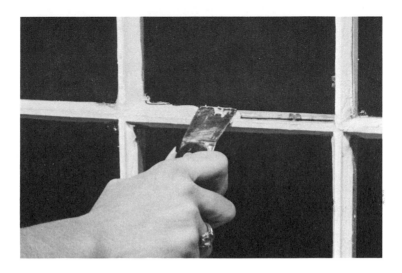

Press on glazing compound all around the glass, as shown.

To apply glazing compound correctly, first press it in all along the side of the frame. Then draw it smooth with a putty knife, as shown.

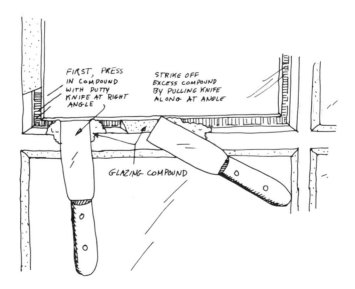

FIRST, PRESS IN COMPOUND WITH PUTTY KNIFE AT RIGHT ANGLE

STRIKE OFF EXCESS COMPOUND BY PULLING KNIFE ALONG AT ANGLE

GLAZING COMPOUND

Then, proceed to do the other sides of the window, one by one, as just described. Let the compound dry for half a day, then paint it and the rest of the window.

If the glass breaks on a Sunday or other time when you can't replace it, you can make temporary repair with a piece of cardboard or plastic wrap. Simply tape the material over the window—it's better than nothing.

7

Repairs
Outside the House

Many repairs on the outside of the house require a bit too much physical strength for a woman to undertake. But there are a few important ones that can be done.

Crumbling Brick Mortar

As time goes by, mortar—the stuff between bricks—loosens and crumbles. The holes should be filled for good looks and to stop further deterioration.

To do the job, five tools are required, all available at hardware stores or building supply dealers(see your Yellow Pages): a pointing trowel (about $1.50), a hammer, a wire brush (about 75¢), and a jointer (about $1.30)—which is a special tool (it looks like a very thin trowel) for smoothing the mortar out after it is applied—and a three-quarter-inch cold chisel (about $1.00).

For the hole filler, a premixed mortar is best. This is a powder that comes in 10- to 80-pound bags. All you do

Remove unsound loose material with a cold chisel. Wear plastic sunglasses to protect your eyes.

is add water in the amount specified on the label, and mix. Sakrete is one brand name.

First, use the cold chisel and hammer to chip out all unsound mortar—the stuff that's barely hanging on. To protect your eyes against flying chips, wear a pair of plastic sunglasses.

Follow this by wire-brushing out all loose, crumbly material.

Next, open up the bag of mortar mix and pour the powder out on a piece of plywood, cardboard, or butcher paper. Thoroughly mix it with the trowel, as if you were blending flour and sugar. When it is all the same color, shape it into a little hill and make a hole in the center. Add a little water. Mix this with the powder fully. Gradually add more water until you've added all specified on the label. (You can also mix the mortar in a plastic pail.)

Wet down the area to be repaired with water, then pack freshly mixed mortar into the holes. Prepared mortar mix is best. All you do is add water in specified proportion, as if you were mixing flour.

Carry the fresh mortar to the bricks in a pail or pan. Plop a soaking rag against the holey area to get it good and wet, then scoop out some mortar on the tip of the trowel and force it into a hole. Keep putting mortar in until the hole is overfilled a fraction of an inch; while filling, poke at the mortar to remove air pockets.

Let the mortar alone for about five minutes, then draw the jointer over it to shape and smooth it so it looks like the surrounding mortar.

If you smear any mortar on the bricks, clean it off right away, using the wire brush and water.

Every day for a week after the job, give the patches a half-minute light spray from your garden hose. This enables the mortar to "cure" properly.

Incidentally, you won't know how much mortar you'll need until you start the job. So buy a 45-pound bag at first. Hardware stores and building supply dealers carry it. A 45-pound bag costs about $1.50.

Give the mortar a few minutes to "set up"—solidify—then draw a jointer over it to smooth it out to match the surrounding mortar. You can also use a trowel.

Cracks in Concrete

Concrete steps, walks, and driveways commonly develop cracks. Indeed, sometimes it seems as if there is no such thing as concrete without cracks.

At any rate, the repair is as easy as filling mortar holes. You use the same tools except that you don't need the jointer.

Start by digging out all unsound (loose) material with your cold chisel and hammer. Brush out as much material as you can with a wire brush.

Douse the crack with a fine spray from the hose. Fill the crack immediately.

The best filler for concrete is sand mix. Like mortar mix, it comes in premixed form to which you add water. Start with an 11-pound bag. (Cost is about $1.25.)

Pour the mix onto a piece of plywood, cardboard, or

butcher paper. Blend it with the trowel, make a little hill, poke a hole in the middle, and add a little water. Blend this water in, then the rest specified on the bag. Or, as with mortar, mix it all in a pail.

Force the fresh mix down into the crack, poking it frequently to remove air pockets. Fill the crack completely, then smooth it level with the surrounding concrete by drawing the bottom of the trowel across it.

Place a piece of burlap or an old towel on the patch. Wet the cloth with a fine spray from your garden hose. Each day for a couple of days, wet it down the same way. A loose brick or board will hold the burlap or towel in place.

For a little more money, you can get a product called Megasil (it's available at hardware stores, building supply stores, and lumberyards) that's more convenient and easier to work with than sand mix. Megasil comes in 10-pound bags and is mixed the same way as sand mix. But it doesn't have to be kept damp for a few days after application. It is also said to be stronger than sand mix. A 10-pound bag costs about $4.

Clogged Gutters

All that's really required to do this job is the wherewithal to get up on a ladder, and somebody to help you maneuver the ladder. If you feel queasy about the whole thing, don't do it. Nervousness could cause an accident.

If you do go up, make sure you use a good ladder. If you're getting a new one, get aluminum—it's light, yet strong. A 16-foot extension ladder can handle the jobs on most homes. Also, while you're up there, have someone hold the ladder at the bottom while you're at the top; or put something heavy against the bottom of the ladder on the outside. Then there's no real chance the bottom can slide out. (Caution: Be careful using an aluminum ladder near power lines.)

Gutters usually become clogged in spring and autumn from leaves, twigs, bird nests, and assorted debris. If you don't clear them, collected water can make the gutter sag. Also the water may back up and run down inside house walls.

Lean the ladder against the house, or against the gutter if that's necessary for proper ladder placement. Sight down the gutter. Wherever you see debris, move the ladder into position and scoop it out with a garden trowel or other implement. You can drop the material in a plastic bucket hooked to the top rung (with a piece of hanger wire) or simply drop it on the ground and clean it up later.

Proceed around the house as above. When all the blockages are cleared, lug a garden hose up the ladder and run water into each gutter to clear it completely. If the water does not run quickly out the downspout, it means the downspout is clogged.

Try to clear it with a steady stream of water from the hose. If this doesn't do the job, you can use a "snake"—the same thing you use to clear a clogged sink drain. Simply feed the pointed end of the snake down into the downspout. When you hit a blockage, move the snake up and down to shake it loose. Follow by shooting a stream of water down the spout. For greater water force, you can hold your forefinger halfway over the hose nozzle.

Leaking Gutters

Gutters made from galvanized metal eventually develop leaks; aluminum ones don't, and wood doesn't. At any rate, experience should have told you where the leaks are. If you don't know, wait until the first rainy day, then grab your umbrella and go outside and look. Note where the leaks are. First sunny day, repair them.

To repair a hole in a galvanized gutter, you use roof-

To make a repair in a metal gutter, scour away all rust with wire brush. Apply a layer of roofing cement, lay on a burlap patch, then add a fresh application of roofing cement. Get the cement smooth—not bumpy—so water can flow freely.

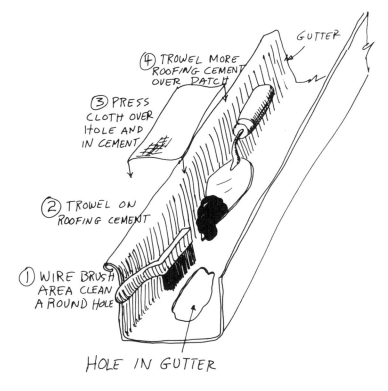

ing cement and ordinary burlap. (Your local food market should have some.) Sears sells roofing cement for around $1.50 a gallon, all you'll need for the job.

First, use a wire brush to remove all rust around the hole, down to absolutely clean metal. To make sure you get it all off, follow the wire brushing by rubbing with emery cloth, a special sandpaper for metal. It is available at hardware stores.

Using a spatula, scraper, or trowel, lay a good glob of the cement over the hole, and spread it three inches on either side of the hole. The coating should be about a quarter-inch thick.

Cut a piece of burlap as wide as the cement, and press firmly and flatly into the cement. Cover the burlap with another thin coat of cement, overlapping the edges about an inch each. The reason you get the burlap and cement flat and smooth is so water can flow freely by.

If the leak is at a joint—where gutter sections join— use the same procedure as for a hole.

Hole in a Blacktop Driveway

If you have some holes in your blacktop driveway, you can repair them easily. The job is done with ready-to-use cold mix asphalt patching compound, which comes in various size heavy bags. Unless you've taken up weight lifting between trips to the beauty parlor, however, better have the store (hardware store or building materials supply) deliver it smack dab on your driveway where you're going to use it. Sakrete is one good brand. The cost is about $2.00 for a 66-pound bag.

First, shovel out all loose rocks and debris from the hole. If the hole is more than six inches wide and four or five inches deep, place at the bottom a large rock (you might get one at a local lot or from nearby woods). This serves as your base, and conserves the patcher.

Open the blacktop bag and scoop out a shovelful. Pour it into the hole. Do this until the hole is filled to within about an inch of the top. Use the end of a hefty board or the back of the shovel to compact (pat down hard) the blacktop; it's fairly soft, so you shouldn't have any trouble. When it seems thoroughly compacted, add more blacktop mix, this time filling a half-inch higher than the surrounding driveway surface.

Now compact some more. You can do this with a board or shovel, but it's easier and you'll do a better job with your car. Simply drive one wheel back and forth over it until the patch is level with the rest of the driveway.

Prepared blacktop mix is best for holes in a blacktop driveway. It comes ready to use. Overfill the hole about half an inch.

Then pack it down with the end of a board and drive over it with a car wheel to compact it.

Leaking Rubber Hose

Some books have long recommended stopping a leak in rubber garden hose by wrapping tape over the hole. Actually, this is about as effective as sticking your finger in a leaking dike. The pressure of the water eventually forces it off.

The repair should be made with a thing called a clincher mender. This is a brass tube, in the middle of which are encircling teeth. You can get one in a hardware store for about 40¢. Show your dealer the hose so he'll give you the right size.

First, use a single-edge razor blade or a sharp knife to cut out the section of the hose with the hole. Keep your cuts straight up and down (not slanted). Slip one end of the clincher mender into one section of the hose and hammer down the teeth so they bite into the rubber and

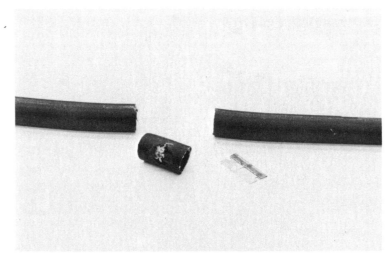

Begin the repair of a rubber hose by cutting out the bad part with a
razor blade. Keep the cuts even.

The repair is made with a device called a clincher mender.

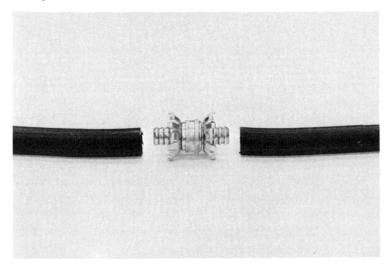

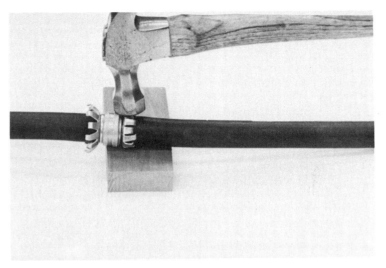

To attach it, stick one tube of the device into one end of the hose,
then hammer down the prongs. Then do the same on the other side.

are flat. Slip the other end of the device into the other
section of hose and hammer down those teeth.

Leaking Plastic Hose

Tape won't stop a leak in plastic hose either. Here, as
with rubber hose, you use a clincher mender, but one
made of sheet brass rather than pure brass. The repair is
made the same way. However, if you have difficulty
sticking the tube into the end of the cut hose you can
soften the hose by dipping it in warm water. Cost of a
clincher mender for plastic hose repair is about $1.00.

Hole in Screening

Hail to the genius who invented screening! He made
the openings in the screening small enough so bugs can't
get in but big enough so cooling breezes can, and you
can see through the screen.

Frequently, however, holes show up that weren't part of the original design. And before you know it you've got tiny, unwelcome visitors.

The repair depends on whether you have metal or plastic screening, and the extent of the damage.

If wires in metal screen are misaligned, making a "hole," push them back into position with the point of an awl or icepick.

A small hole—less than a quarter-inch wide—in either type of screening can be plugged with a drop of airplane glue or household cement, such as Duco. For this repair there's no need to take the screen down.

For a bigger hole on metal screening, you can buy a ready-to-use patch (available at hardware stores). This is simply a small rectangle of screening with hooks on the ends.

Take the screen down and place it on a flat surface. Place the hole over a small block of wood and tap hole edges with a hammer to flatten them. Place the patch over the hole and thread the hooked ends through the screening. Turn the screen over, placing the patch on the small wood block (or a book). Tap the patch hooks with a hammer so they flatten and grip the screening. That's it.

For a hole in plastic screening, you need to obtain a piece of scrap screening. If you don't have a piece, try a hardware store; they sell it loose.

Anyway, cut a patch about a quarter-inch bigger than the hole. Squeeze out a line of household cement around the edge of the patch. Press the patch in place over the hole and hold it there for a few minutes, then release it and let it dry completely.

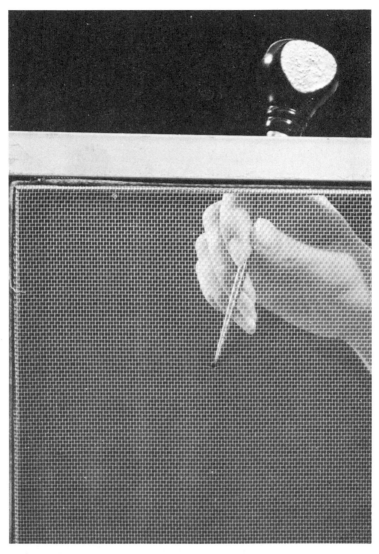

If a screen has a hole just because the screen wires are a little misaligned, put them back in place with pointed tool, such as an icepick.

A very small hole can be plugged with a drop of airplane glue.

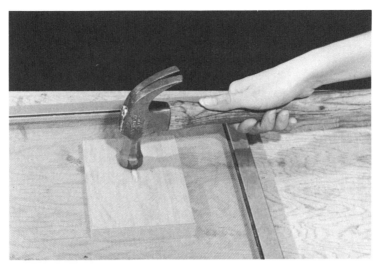

If a hole in a metal screen is too big for glue, a ready-made screen patch is the answer. First, flatten out the edges of the hole by tapping them with a hammer.

Press the patch onto the hole, letting its hooked edges pass through the screen wire. Then turn the screen over, lay it on a wood block, and tap the hooked edges of the patch to flatten them and make them grip the wire.

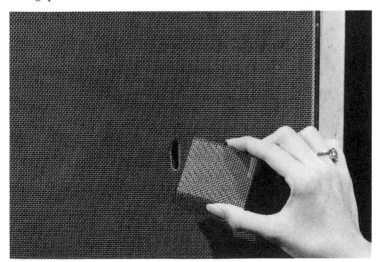

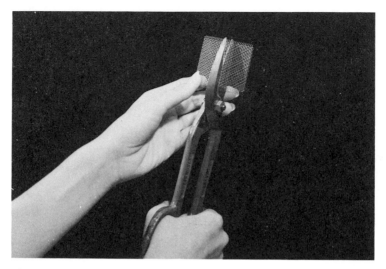

If you want to make two patches, or a smaller patch, you can cut the patch with shears.

Ripped Screen

If there's a big gash in a screen or it's otherwise extensively damaged, the only repair is replacing the screening. Replacement procedures vary, depending on what the screening material is and what kind of frame it is set into.

If you're replacing metal screening in metal frames, follow this procedure:

With a screwdriver, pry up a corner of the spline—the long thin strip of rubber that holds the screening edges in the grooves around the frame; pull it free with your fingers. Lift out the screening and discard it.

New metal screening is available at hardware stores and costs about 8¢ a square foot. To install it, you need a utility knife (about $1.25) or a razor blade, plus a special screening tool that has a little metal wheel at each end, one with a concave surface and the other convex. You can get along without it, but it only costs about $2.50 and makes the job very much easier. If you're doing more than one screen, it's definitely worth the price.

First, cut a new piece of screening two inches bigger on all sides than the screen frame. Lay the piece on the frame squarely so there is equal overlap all around. Using the convex wheel on the screening tool, tuck the screen into the grooves in the frame. Use short strokes.

Next, using the concave wheel, roll a piece of spline in one side. If the existing spline is in bad shape, you can get new spline at a hardware store. The advantage of using old spline is that it is already cut to the correct lengths. With spline in one end, pull the screening taut

A screen may require replacement. For replacing metal screening, start by lifting up one corner of the spline. Then pull it all out with your fingers and discard the screen (or save it to make patches).

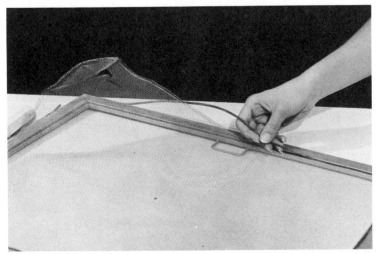

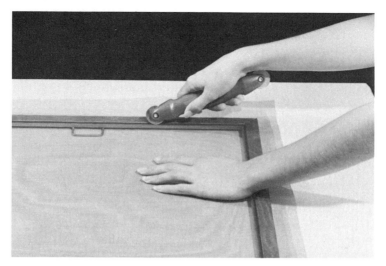

Cut a piece of screening (use shears) at least two inches wider all
around than the frame. Center the screen on the frame, then, to tuck
the screen into the grooves, use short strokes of the convex wheel on
a special screening tool you can buy.

Use the concave wheel on the tool to install spline. Pull the screen
taut to the opposite side and repeat this procedure. Then do one long
side, pull the screen taut to other side, and do that.

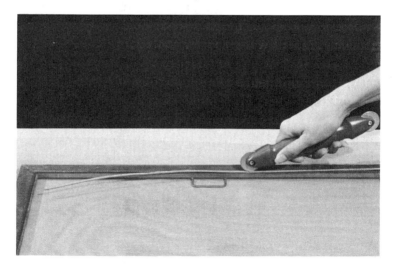

to the opposite side and roll another piece of spline in that groove. Insert spline in one end, pull the screening taut to the opposite end, and insert spline there. Using the metal frame as a guide, trim excess screening with a utility knife or a razor blade.

If the screen uses lengths of rigid metal instead of rubber spline, follow the same steps as described above, but use a tapered block of wood instead of the screening tool to set the strips in their grooves.

To replace fiber glass (plastic) screening in metal frames, remove the spline as above, but cut the new piece of screening only as big as the frame. Center it on the frame and then, to get it taut, tuck it in at all four corners with one-inch lengths of spline or dowels (the latter are thin round sticks available at lumberyards). Then replace the spline (whether rubber or metal) in this order: one side, one end, the other side, and the final end. In other words, clockwise or counterclockwise. Trim the excess as for metal screening; pull taut as you go.

Instead of grooves and spline to hold screening in place, wooden-frame screens use tacked—or stapled-on—strips of wood. To replace metal screening in wooden frames, first use a putty knife (or a butter knife or screwdriver) to pry free the strips.

Cut a piece of screening that's an inch bigger on all sides than the old screening. Square up the new piece on the frame. Use a staple gun or tacks to fasten the screening to one side; place the tacks or staples two inches apart. Fold over the overlap and tack it down, placing the tacks between the ones already in. (Incidentally, Swingline sells a staple gun designed for women for $7.00 or so.)

If your screen uses a metal instead of a rubber spline, a tapered block of wood can be used for tucking the screen in and tapping in the spline.

With the screening in, trim it with a single-edge razor or utility knife. Run the point of the knife against the edge of the frame to guide it.

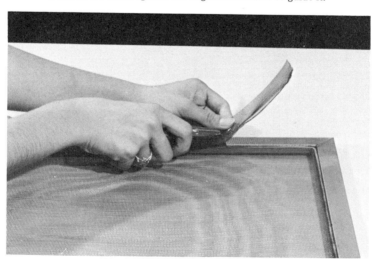

For wooden-frame screens, start by lifting up the molding that goes over the edges of the screening.

Take out the old screen and cut a new piece as large as the frame.

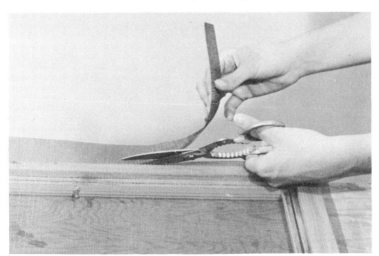

Staple or tack one side of the screen to the frame. One staple every two inches is good. When one short side is done, staple the piece to an adjacent long side, then a short side, and finally a long side, pulling the screen taut as you go.

Fold over excess screening all around and staple it in place, putting staples in between previous ones. Replace the molding, tacking it in place.

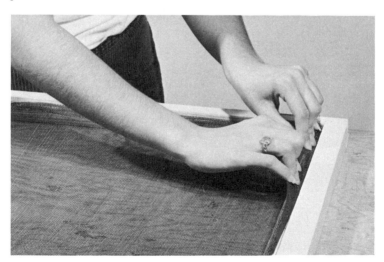

Pull the screening taut to the opposite side and repeat the fastening procedure. Then attach the screening to one end, pull the material to the opposite end, and tack it in place. Then replace the molding, either with the nails that came out when you pried the strips free or with some new ones of the same size.

Installing fiber glass screening in wooden frames is done the same way as if you were putting in metal screening, but fasten it on in clockwise or counterclockwise order, starting with a side.

All the above may sound hopelessly complicated, but it's really very easy. When you have all the materials and tools in front of you, you'll see this.

8

Miscellaneous Maladies

A wide variety of problems that show up in a house can't be easily classified—except under "Trouble." Here's a roundup of these pests and how to handle them.

Squeaky Floor

This is caused by one or more loose floorboards— usually just one. When you step on the board, it bends more than it should and rubs against adjacent boards— the rubbing produces the squeak. Or one board is bowed (warped).

The answer is to nail the board down tightly so it can't move. You can use a 2½-inch finishing nail or, for an even tighter job, a special nail called a spiral-fluted flooring nail. This has a surface that is partially fluted, or grooved, and has greater holding power.

First press on the various boards to find out which one is squeaking. When you discover it, drive a nail in at the approximate point where you figure it's bending. (If

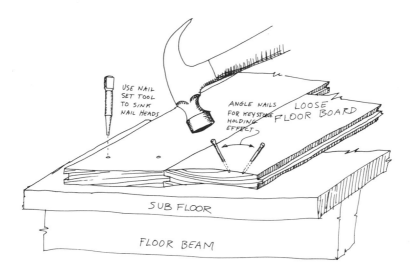

USE NAIL
SET TOOL
TO SINK
NAIL HEADS

ANGLE NAILS
FOR KEYSTONE
HOLDING
EFFECT

LOOSE
FLOOR BOARD

SUB FLOOR

FLOOR BEAM

If necessary, nail the loose board down. If it can't move, it can't
squeak. Drive nails in at the angle shown. Drive nailheads below surface with a nailset and fill little depressions with wood putty to
match the floor. Sand smooth.

you don't get it exactly, no sweat.) For greater holding
power, drive the nail in at a slight angle—about as much
as the Leaning Tower of Pisa leans.

Step on the board. Still squeaks? Okay, drive another
nail in a little way (two inches from the other), also an-
gling it. Test for squeaking again. *Still* squeak? If so, drive
another nail, also angled, about two inches from the first
nail you drove in.

With the nails in, take a nailset (a tool that looks like
an extra thick nail with a small, blunt end) and drive the
heads of the nails a little bit below the surface. Then fill
the depressions with wood putty the color of the wood,
and sand smooth. This will hide the nailheads. Of course,
if you have a rug or other covering on the floor this won't
be necessary.

(Incidentally, when using the hammer, hold it down

near the end and, every time you hit the nail, flip your
wrist as if you were cracking a whip. Your arm has very
little to do with the force you can apply to the nail. I
learned how to hold a hammer the hard way, about 15
years ago when I was doing construction work. The fore-
man, a laconic Southerner, observed me holding a hammer several inches from the end. He asked me for the
hammer, drew a rule mark on it a couple of inches from
the end and asked for my saw. As he was poised to cut
off the end of the hammer I said, "Wait, why are you
doing that?" "Shoot, boy," he answered, "you don't
need this last two inches. You held the hammer up here."
Then everybody roared. Except me. I reddened.)

You may be able to silence the squeak without nails.
Just squirt some powdered graphite between the boards.
When the board rubs, the lubrication prevents it from
making noise.

When a floor squeaks, spray powdered graphite in the cracks on
either side of the loose board. Sometimes this will silence it.

Hole in Vinyl

Until relatively recently, if vinyl or vinyl-covered furniture, luggage, clothing, or other items got torn, there was not much you could do about it except apply some colored tape to prevent the tear from spreading and hide it as much as possible. Now there are a number of vinyl kits available that enable you to make a virtually invisible repair.

One of the best is put out by Red Devil. The cost is about $1.95 per kit.

To use it, start by trimming off the edge of the tear with scissors or a razor, removing frayed parts. Place a piece of vinyl fabric that comes in the kit behind the hole, as you would place a patch you were sewing on. This may be simple to do in the case of clothing. If you are repairing something like a kitchen chair, where the vinyl is tautly stretched, you'll have to work the material carefully down into and behind the hole.

With the vinyl backing in place, apply the liquid vinyl. It is available in black, white, clear, blue, green, brown, red, and yellow. If necessary, you can mix one or more colors to match the shade needed.

Next, select one of the "graining papers" that come in the kit. These are pieces of material, each with a different texture, to match the textures of most vinyls, from smooth to fairly deep-textured.

Press the appropriate one into the wet vinyl, then apply a warm household iron directly over the tear. This fuses everything together. After a few seconds, peel off the graining paper and the repair is done.

Incidentally, if you want to refurbish vinyl items, the

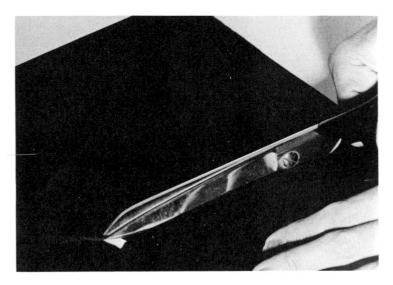

Vinyl is easily repaired with a commercially available kit. You just cut out damaged part and apply liquid patcher which is then textured to match surrounding vinyl.

same company puts out liquid vinyls in different colors that you can paint on.

Dirty Walls

In this day and age, walls can get awfully dirty, very quickly. To save yourself a good deal of elbow grease in washing them, start at the bottom of the wall and work up. If you wash from the top, dirty water can streak down, and it will be difficult to remove the streak marks. If you're washing plasterboard walls, don't use a lot of water. Plasterboard has a paper covering, and it could lift.

Hole in Wallboard

Wallboard, also known as sheetrock and plasterboard, is the most popular wall and ceiling material in new homes and apartments. Usually, it doesn't develop cracks like plaster, but an errant foot of a dancer or the corner of a piece of furniture can poke a hole in it.

To repair the damage, first use a pencil and a ruler to draw a triangle around the hole; the triangle should be just big enough so all of the hole is inside it.

Use a keyhole saw (at hardware stores for $1.00 or so) or a loose hacksaw blade to cut out the wallboard outlined by the triangle, *i.e.,* the hole and material around it. Make your cuts slanted so that when you look at the edges you can see their slope, just as you would

Wallboard can be repaired by cutting a patch to fit hole, securing it with joint compound. Note slanted edges on the patch.

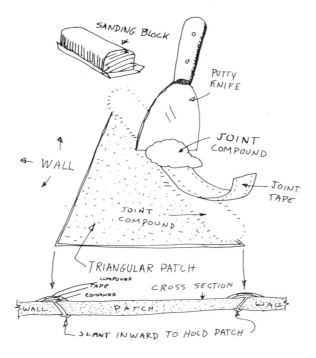

when looking down at London Broil from which you have cut slices.

Obtain a small piece of plasterboard (at building supply stores or lumberyards), the same thickness as the existing material (bring a waste piece to show to your dealer). Cut a patch to fit the triangle, this time slanting the edges so they fit snugly into the wall triangle edges.

Mix up a batch or joint compound (available at hardware stores) and use a scraper or putty knife or spatula to smear the compound into the edges of the patch as if you were buttering bread. Press the patch into place in the wall and skim off the compound that squeezes out, with a scraper or putty knife.

Apply a very thin coat—as thin as you can make it— of joint compound over the edges of the patch. Cut and press pieces of perforated joint tape (also available at hardware stores) over the edges into the compound. Apply more compound over the tape. This coat should also be very thin and as smooth as you can make it. If it's bumpy, the patch will be noticeable.

If the wall is painted, first touch up the patch with a coat of the finish paint you're going to use, let dry, then paint the entire wall. If you just paint the patch, it will stand out like a sore thumb, even if you use the same paint that was originally used.

The above repair is for holes that are, say, up to six or seven inches wide. If you've got something bigger than that, it is better to take the whole panel down and replace it. I would say that this is a bit too much for someone new at the plasterboard game.

Hole in Plaster

Plaster is a popular material in apartments. Unlike wallboard, which is applied in solid sheets, plaster is applied wet with a trowel. If you don't know what you have, rap on a wall with your knuckles. Wallboard sounds hollow, plaster solid.

Plaster commonly develops cracks and holes. The repair technique depends on what you're dealing with.

If a wall or ceiling has so-called "hairline" cracks—they look like veins—the first step is to widen and deepen them so the repair filler used can get a better grip.

If you can, get the now old-fashioned beer can opener with a hooked end. Draw the hooked part of this along inside the crack, digging deeply as you go. If you don't have an opener, you can use a screwdriver or scraper.

For filler, use plaster of Paris. A five-pound bag (enough for all rooms in the average house) costs about 60¢. Pour some plaster in an empty coffee can or similar container and add a little water. Using a scraper, mix this up. Gradually add more until the plaster is soft and workable without being soupy. To every coffee-can full you mix, add a teaspoon of ordinary vinegar. This will triple the setting (hardening) time of the plaster, which ordinarily would be only about 10 minutes.

Wet the crack(s) down by sponging water in with a soaking wet rag. Using a 3½-inch wide scraper with a flexible blade (a good scraper costs around $1.75 in paint stores), force the plaster into the crack and smooth it out level with the surrounding wall.

Try to get the plaster perfectly smooth with the scraper. If you try to sandpaper it smooth later, you won't succeed. After smoothing with the scraper (try to use as few strokes as possible), draw a folded, soaking wet rag across it as a final smoothing process.

If you have a hole to repair that's less than two inches wide, follow this procedure. First, remove all loose crumbly material with a scraper. Slop a soaking rag into the hole, wetting it completely.

Mix plaster (don't forget the vinegar) and pack it into the hole until it's three quarters full. Let it dry completely, then fill the hole the rest of the way. Smooth it level with the surrounding wall and wipe extra-smooth with a wet rag.

If a hole is more than two inches wide, clean it out as described above, then stuff—fill it three quarters full— with ordinary steel wool, wedging it in tightly. (This is done because plaster walls commonly have no backing material that the new plaster can stick to--the steel wool becomes the backing). Apply a coat of plaster in the hole that fills it about three quarters of the way; be sure to cover the hole edges. When this dries, fill the hole the rest of the way, smoothing out as before.

Mildew

You can find mildew on the inside or outside of the house, commonly in damp areas. It is a fungus and should be removed for good looks and to stop it from discoloring the surface it's on.

Many people mistake mildew for dirt. To tell the difference, dab a little pure bleach on the discoloration. If the stain disappears, it's probably mildew; if not, it's dirt. Usually, mildew is gray and has a cobweb-like appearance.

You can remove mildew with a homemade solution. To every three quarts of warm water, add two-thirds cup of Soilax, one-third cup of detergent and one quart of household bleach. Wear rubber gloves and scrub the mildew with a scrub brush. A few washings may be necessary to remove it.

Damaged Ceramic Tile

Ceramic tile is one of the toughest building materials available. That's why it's usually used for bathroom walls. However, it is not impervious to damage. It can be scratched, or broken, or chipped, and it can fall out. For good looks and to keep moisture from sneaking through behind the tiles, any that are damaged should be replaced.

This is sometimes easier said than done. You can buy replacement tiles at tile stores, but if the tiles have been up a fair amount of time their original color will have changed slightly and you may not be able to get ones that match. Then again, you might be in luck and get ones that match—or match well enough. At any rate, if you do make the replacement, the main thing to remember is to not damage adjacent tiles.

To get a damaged tile out, use a three-quarter-inch cold chisel (available at hardware stores for about $1.00) and a hammer. Chip away at the corners of the tile. Usually there's a little space under them.

When all the corners are chipped out, slip the chisel under one and lift. The tile should come out easily.

Scrape away all the adhesive on the wall. When it's

all off, apply fresh epoxy adhesive (a two-ounce kit of Devcon epoxy costs about $1.00) around the edges and in the middle of the replacement tile and set it in place. Push it in so it's level with surrounding tiles and has an equal amount of space around its edges.

Or, even easier and cheaper, just mix up some plaster of Paris and set the tile in this. When the adhesive or plaster of Paris is dry, use your finger to fill in around the tile with a ready-mixed grout (available in tubes for about 50¢ at hardware stores). Smooth it out with your finger so it (the grout) is shaped like the grout between the other tiles. Finally, take a wet sponge and clean off all grout smeared on the tiles.

Usually, the grout required is white. If you need a colored grout, get the kind that can be tinted with "universal" colors. These are available in small tubes at paint stores.

Crooked Picture

When a picture falls out of line, it usually means that it was not made properly—one side is heavier than the other. You should, of course, straighten it out—but fix it so it can't move again.

First, straighten the picture on the wall; note the point on the wire or cord where it balances. If a wire is used, crimp it at the balance point. If you use cord, make a little loop at this point.

Also, cut a pencil eraser in half and glue one piece (use rubber cement) to each bottom back corner of the frame. This will help stop the frame from moving and will allow free air circulation—when you take the picture down there won't be a dirty outline of it on the wall.

Split Utensil Handles

I'm talking here about the split wooden handles on ladles, spatulas, big forks, and the like.

The repair is made with epoxy glue. As mentioned, you can get a two-ounce kit under the Devcon brand for about $1.00. Like other glues, it is available at hardware stores.

If the handle is pretty badly split—finish it. Pull it apart into two pieces. Check each part to make sure it is dry and clean, especially of grease.

Following label directions, apply the epoxy to each piece of the handle. Push the parts together and tie tightly with thin cord.

When the glue is dry, pick off the cord and remove glue that has oozed out of the split, using medium-grade sandpaper. Wipe away all dust, then immerse the handle in a can (like a big frozen orange juice can) filled with a quality polyurethane varnish, such as Sears makes. A pint, enough for the job, costs about $1.50.

Let the handle stand in the can for a half hour, then pull it out and let excess varnish drain off for a few minutes. Then turn the utensil over and prop it up until the varnish dries.

During drying, some varnish will run down onto the metal part of the utensil. This can easily be peeled off later. But leave a little of it at the point where wood meets metal, as a seal against water penetration.

Worn Resilient Tile

Resilient tile gets its name from the fact that it has some "give"—it depresses when you step on it. If one gets badly worn, cracked, or chipped you should replace it. There are six or seven different kinds, and repair methods vary according to the type being replaced. If you don't know what kind you have, you can try all methods until one works.

Your first job, of course, is to remove the bad tile. If you have vinyl asbestos or asphalt tile, you can do this with heat. First put a damp rag on the tile, then place an iron, at its hottest setting, on the rag. As you apply heat, pry up the tile at the edges with a putty knife. Usually the tile will curl up and can be removed easily.

Apply the new tile. The existing adhesive may still be

The way to loosen a damaged vinyl asbestos or asphalt tile is with heat. Lay a damp towel on the tile, then apply a hot iron to the towel.

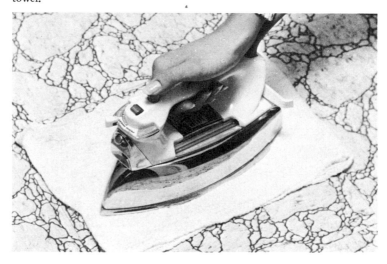

To remove a vinyl or rubber tile, cut it out. First cut deeply all around it with a sharp linoleum knife or a utility knife. Then work it out with a chisel and a hammer.

good. All you do is lay the new tile in place and roll it on securely with a rolling pin. If you can't use the old adhesive, use epoxy.

Vinyl and rubber tiles are removed without heat. Using a curved linoleum knife, a single-edge razor blade, or a utility knife, cut deeply around the edge of the tile—in the seams between it and adjacent tiles.

Using a chisel (a cold chisel is good) and a hammer, start removing the damaged tile. Take care not to damage the edges of adjacent tiles. If necessary, you can chop into the center of the tile, and work toward the edges. When you've got all the pieces out, take off any adhesive remaining on the floor, and high spots of any sort. Also, fill holes with wood putty—Durham's is one good brand. The idea is to get a level surface so the new tile will be level with surrounding tiles.

If you don't have a spare replacement tile around—

and you probably don't—you may have a problem. You may not be able to get a matching replacement tile, because the existing ones may have discolored.

If this is the case, consider taking up four or five tiles in a row, or four tiles in adjacent rows, and installing tiles of a contrasting color as an accent touch. This works well in front of a kitchen sink or in the middle of a room.

Felt Lamp Pads Fall Off

If you examine the bottoms of lamps, candlesticks, vases, and the like you'll see that they're covered by felt pads. This is to keep the item from scratching furniture.

With time, these pads either fall off or become matted with dust, furniture wax, or polish. In either case, replacement is called for.

First, carefully peel off the old felt in one piece and use it as a pattern for cutting a new piece. (Felt is available at hobby stores, such as Tandy Craft). If there is no old felt, or the existing material is badly damaged, or you rip it during removal, cut a new piece a half-inch larger all around than the base of the item.

Apply glue to the bottom of the item and set it on the felt. You can use white glue for metal, wood, glass or really, anything, but household cement (such as Duco) works better for glass and metal bottoms. Use the glue sparingly—too much and it'll soak through the felt. Also, if you use household cement, don't set the item on a varnished or painted surface. The glue vapors can damage these finishes.

If you had the exact-size piece of felt needed, the job is done. If you have overlapping felt, trim it off with a single-edge razor blade or scissors—whichever works best, depending on the shape of the particular item.

If you're replacing items with "feet"—such as lamps with animal paws—use a double layer of felt. Follow the procedure for the first layer as described above. Stick the second layer on with just a tiny bit of adhesive.

Torn Shower Curtain

The easiest way to repair a torn shower curtain is with cloth adhesive tape, such as Mystic Tape. This is available in a wide variety of styles and colors. It also comes in transparent form.

If the tear is on the edge of the curtain, cut a piece of tape that's twice as long as the tear, plus two inches. With bleach, clean the area around the tear—both sides—to eliminate mildew. Let it dry. Center the tape on the edge of the tear and press it down into place on both sides; it should overlap the tear an inch or so on each side.

If the tear is in another part of the curtain, cut two pieces of tape, each a couple of inches longer than the tear. Clean the area—on both sides—with bleach. Let it dry, then apply one piece of tape to one side, centering it so it overlaps the tear an inch on each end. Do the same on the other side.

For a really inconspicuous repair, you can use a patch taken from the shower curtain itself. A patch can usually be cut from excess along the side or bottom edges.

Clean the area as before. Position the patch on the tear so its pattern or design blends with that on the curtain, as if you were patching wallpaper. Secure the patch with plastic cement. One brand is Duco; it is available at hardware stores and costs under $1.00. Double the drying time given on the label directions. If they say 12 hours, make it 24.

When a shade doesn't go up, take it off the window. Unroll it all the way down, then tightly rewind it halfway up.

Window Shade Trouble

For such a simple device, a shade can have a surprising number of difficulties. Following are problems you may encounter and how to handle them.

(1) *Shade doesn't go up all the way.* This is usually caused by a lack of tension in a little spring inside the shade roller. To get more tension, pull the shade down about two thirds of the way. Remove it from the window, and roll it up tightly around the roller. Hold it tightly rolled up and replace it in the window. Try it. It should work properly.

(2) *Shade flies up when you pull it up.* This is caused by the little spring's having too much tension. Cure: Raise the shade as high as it will go, remove it from the window, then unroll it by hand halfway down. Replace the shade in the window. Try it. Still too fast? Repeat the procedure.

If a shade does not go up easily, spray some powdered graphite into the ends of the shade.

(3) *Shade won't stay in place when you pull it down but rolls back up.* Take the shade down and look on the end of the roller that has the little spring on it—that is, the end that has a little metal bar sticking out with little gear-like affairs around it. Check everything there for dirt. If you see any, brush and wipe it away with a rag. Then, whether you had dirt or not, squirt some powdered graphite into the end, covering everything. Powdered graphite comes in small tubes and is commonly available at hardware stores.

Loose Toilet Paper Dispenser

When a small fixture, such as a toilet paper dispenser, is attached to a plasterboard wall with screws, it invariably comes loose. Reason: Plasterboard is simply too thin a material to enable a screw to get a good bite.

If such an item becomes loose, discard the screws

and get a pair of five-eighth-inch "Molly" bolts, a device specifically designed for use with plasterboard. Mollies cost about 40¢ a pair; hardware stores carry them.

With the dispenser removed, use a nail or screw to make the existing screwholes twice the size they were—big enough so the Molly bolt can fit through.

Push the Mollies into the holes. With a screwdriver, tighten the screws in each Molly. As you do, you'll feel pressure or resistance. This is because the wings on the Molly are opening up and pulling against the back of the wall.

When the screws have been tightened all the way, unscrew them. The socket parts will stay in the wall. Align the holes on the fixture over the Mollies and reinsert the

A good device for fastening things on plasterboard walls is a "Molly." To rehang a loose toilet paper dispenser, enlarge the original screwholes with the end of a Molly or a nail. Then turn the screw in the Molly to the right. As you do, you'll feel it tightening.

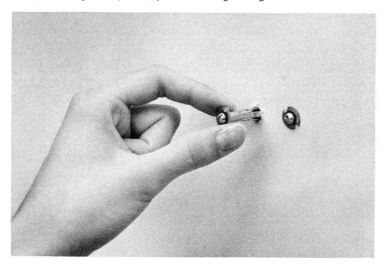

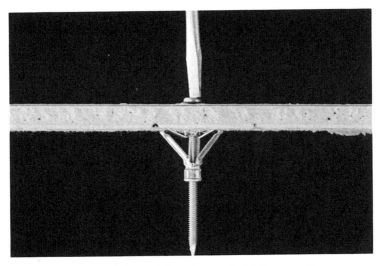

This is because, behind the wall, the wings on the Molly are pulling up tight every time you turn.

When you can't tighten anymore, unscrew the screws. The other parts automatically stay in the wall.

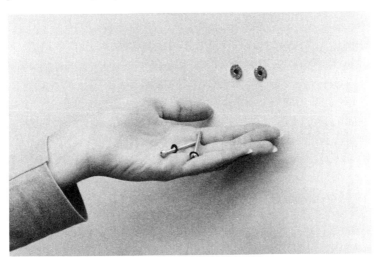

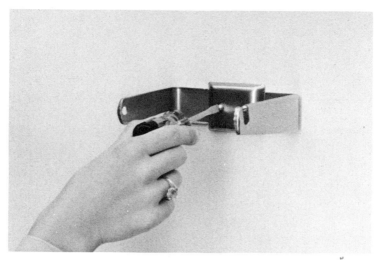

Then simply align the holes on the dispenser over the parts in the wall, reinsert the screws, and tighten them.

screws. Tighten the screws, and the job's done—and will last as long as the wall.

Damaged Bathtub Calk

Calk is the material used to seal the calk seam between the top of the bathtub and the wall. Eventually, it cracks or falls out. To prevent water from getting down behind the tub, the calk should be replaced. One good type of replacement is silicone calk. This stays flexible and resists cracking very well. One brand is Devcon Tub and Tile Sealer; this costs about 90¢ for a four-ounce tube and is commonly available at hardware stores. It comes in a tube like a toothpaste tube and is easy to apply.

Before applying the calk, clean out all the cracked, blackened, or otherwise deteriorated calk. Use a screwdriver or a putty knife. Don't leave any crumbs.

With this done, proceed to apply the new stuff. To use it, simply squeeze the tube. The calk squirts out slowly from its thin spout. As it does, draw the spout

To seal off an opening between the tub and the wall, squeeze out a line of calk. Smooth it with a wet finger or a spoon handle.

along the tub/wall seam. When you've got the seam completely filled in with a solid line of calk, smooth it out with a wet forefinger or a spoon handle. Let it dry. Follow the label for drying time before using the shower or bathtub.

Loose Toilet Seat

Every toilet seat is held to the toilet itself by means of nuts and bolts. When the nuts become loose, the seat is loose.

If the seat is loose, look in the back of the toilet. See the nuts? Tighten them with a pair of pliers, an adjustable wrench, or a monkey wrench, and the problem is solved.

Chipped Porcelain

Washing machines, refrigerators, sinks, and other kitchen appliances and fixtures are coated with porcelain, because it is especially hard, easy to clean, and able to

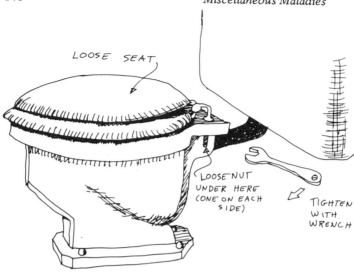

LOOSE SEAT

LOOSE NUT
UNDER HERE
(ONE ON EACH
SIDE)

TIGHTEN
WITH
WRENCH

If a toilet seat becomes loose, look for bolts on the underside at the back of the bowl. Tightening one or both should solve the problem.

take moisture. However, it can chip. When this happens, the metal below is exposed, leaving an unsightly black spot.

A spot like this can be touched up with a special paint specifically made for the job. It is available at paint stores in small bottles and spray cans in every color that appliances and fixtures are made in. For spots, buy a bottle and apply the paint with a Q-Tip or a small brush. If the appliance is badly chipped and you want to refinish it completely, use a can.

Stained Sink

Sometimes a stain in a porcelain sink will resist all efforts of abrasive cleaners to remove it.

When this occurs, you can try soaking it out with

If a stain on a sink won't come off, make a little dam out of clay, between the stain and the drain. Pour pure ammonia on the stain and let it stand overnight.

pure ammonia. To do this, build a little dam of clay or putty around the stain. Pour the ammonia inside the dam. The dam keeps it from running out into the drain. An overnight soaking should take the stain out.

TV Trouble

When something goes wrong with your TV (black and white), chances are 99 out of 100 that a bad tube is causing the trouble. And replacing it is an easy job.

First, disconnect the set. Pull the plug out of the wall. Wait four hours before doing anything; this will eliminate any electrical hazard.

Take the back of the set off. To do this, you'll have to unscrew either regular (single-slot) screws or Phillips screws; the latter have two slots that crisscross. The regular kind can be removed with an ordinary screwdriver. You can use a nail file tip or a table knife point to loosen the Phillips types, if you don't have a Phillips screwdriver.

In addition to screws, the back is attached to the set by a plug; it's plugged in. When you've taken out all the screws, pull straight back on the back and it will unplug.

Somewhere inside the set—on a wall or on the back— will be a tube layout. It may be a piece of pasted-on paper or may be imprinted. This layout is the same thing as a layout of stadium or theater seats, except instead of showing where each seat is located—say seat 4, row A—it shows where the tubes are. So if you see the 5U4 tube located on the front of the diagram, in the middle, you know that's where it will be in the set.

Proceed to remove the tubes by pulling upward on them. If they seem stuck, rock them gently back and forth as you pull up. As you take out each, make a little checkmark on the diagram. If the tubes are especially old, you may have to examine closely to see the number or letter identifications (or both).

Remove all the tubes in the set, including those with little metal guards over them. (Just pull up on the guards to get them off.) The only tubes you don't touch—and can't touch—are those inside a little metal box usually located on the right side of the set. These are the high-voltage tubes. Don't worry about them.

When you have all the tubes out, put them in a paper bag or an empty egg carton and take them down to your radio or TV store. Ask the dealer to test them for you. He has a machine for this, and the job only takes a few minutes. Or, if you like, you can test them yourself, if he has a machine for customer use. It looks complicated,

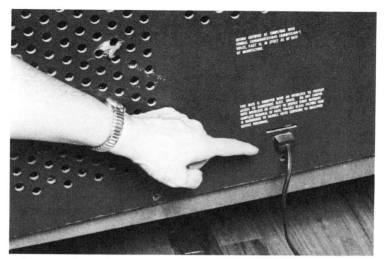

Before taking tubes from a TV set, it is important to take the plug out of the wall. To remove the back, take the screws from it and pull out the plug that is on the back.

Every TV set has a tube layout; it is like a guide to theater seats, showing where each tube is. As you remove the tubes, check each off on the layout.

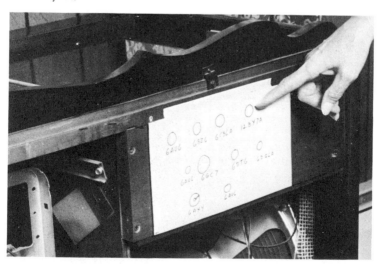

All the tubes can be removed that are in the open and are without danger after being off for four hours, but stay away from the ones that are in a little box in the set. These can give a shock, even when the set is unplugged.

You may have to search for the tube number or letter. It's usually on the side or top of the glass.

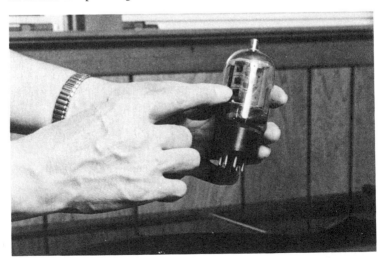

but the directions are there—if you read them you'll be using it in no time flat.

If you had one or more bad tubes, your problem's likely over. With the diagram as a guide, just replace the tubes in the set, substituting new ones for the defective ones, replace the back (don't forget to plug it into the set), and turn the set on. If you still have the trouble, you'll have to call a serviceman.

Broken Crockery

When a piece of china breaks, you might think that that's the end of it. Ten years ago, yes. Not today.

The china can be put back together with epoxy glue, the same glue recommended for a number of other repairs. Its big plus in repairing china is its ability to take heat and water. In fact, you could put the china in boiling water and the glue wouldn't be affected. Epoxy comes colored and clear for repairing glass items.

First, make sure the broken parts of the china are dry and clean. Following label directions, mix epoxy on a piece of aluminum foil and apply it to the broken edges with a toothpick. Push the pieces together and support them in some way so they don't pull apart. Follow label directions for drying time.

Squeaky Stairs

Stairs squeak because the tread, the part you step on, is loose and when pressed down rubs against the board—called a riser—that supports it.

The repair is the same, essentially, as for a loose floorboard.

Have an adult stand on the loose tread to bring it into close contact with the riser. Drive nails through the tread

The best bet for broken crockery is epoxy glue. This comes in two tubes that you mix together before using. The repaired piece can be put in boiling water and the glue will not be affected.

The procedure for stopping a squeak in stairs is essentially the same as correcting a squeaky floor.

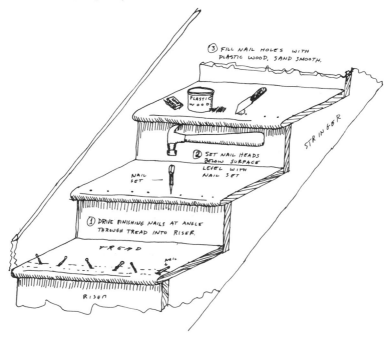

into the riser, following the accompanying sketch for position of nails. You can tell that the nail is going into the riser if you encounter resistance. If the nail suddenly gets easy to drive, you know you've missed it.

Drive the nails even with the tread surface. To hide the holes, tap the nails a little (a sixteenth of an inch) below the surface, using a nailset. Then fill the little holes with wood putty the color of the tread wood.

If the tread is covered by carpeting, you needn't drive the nails below the surface. In fact, if appearance isn't important you can completely forget this step (no pun intended).

Carpet Spots and Stains

High on the list of household traumas is a stained carpet. But the spot can usually be removed by the nonprofessional.

If you don't know what the stain is from, gently blot on a nonflammable dry-cleaning fluid, working from the stain edges toward the center. If this works, dry the carpet quickly and thoroughly by blowing air on the wet area with a vacuum cleaner hose or electric fan. If you can lift the carpet off the floor, this will help drying.

If the dry cleaner doesn't remove the stain, use a clean cloth and blot on a carpet-cleaning detergent. Every now and then, blot up excess fluid with a dry rag. The wetter you get the carpet, the harder it is to dry.

Dry the area again and check. If some stain still remains, use the dry cleaner or detergent again, whichever worked best the first time.

If you know what the stain is from, use the following procedures:

Pet Stains

Sponge the stain with lukewarm water. Blot up as much water as possible with an unstarched cloth. Pat on detergent carpet cleaner; leave it on the stain for 15 minutes. Following this, blot up the solution that remains, and sponge the area with a cloth dipped in lukewarm water. Dry the rug as before.

If the stain doesn't come off, or the rug changes color, you'll have to get it professionally redyed. If the rug has a pattern, you may be able to just get it spot dyed.

Nail Polish

Nail-polish remover can be used here. If the polish is wet, apply a few drops of the remover to it (and only it); an eyedropper is handy. Allow the remover time to mix with the polish; blot up the mixture with a dry rag. Repeat the procedure until the polish is gone, and dry the rug.

If the polish is dry, apply a few drops of the remover. Wait five minutes or so until the remover softens the polish; add more remover if necessary. When polish is soft, scrape off as much as you can with a dull spoon. Apply fresh remover and blot. Keep doing this until stain is gone. Dry the rug.

Acids

Fruit juices can be cleaned by the same method given for removing unidentifiable stains.

Carbolic Acid Disinfectants

These require special treatment. Get to them immediately.

First, flush the acid with water. Blot up any excess with a dry cloth, and repeat. The idea is to dilute the acid. Two or three flushing-blotting treatments should be enough.

Then prepare a solution of one quart of lukewarm water and a teaspoon of baking soda. Using a rag, sponge the stained area. Dry the rug thoroughly and quickly.

Rust

New rust stains can be removed with either detergent or dry-cleaning fluid, as discussed before. If this doesn't work, you'll have to get a professional to remove them.

Ink

If the ink is a permanent type, you won't get it up once it's had time to dry. If it hasn't dried, blot up as much as you can with a dry rag; flush with water and blot up again.

If the ink is the washable type, try the detergent/dry-cleaning method.

Cigarette Burns

The perfect way to remove these is to have the rug rewoven or retufted. But if the burn is slight, you can minimize the eyesore by cutting off the charred tuft ends, then washing with a detergent solution, as previously described.

Collapsing Bed

When a boxspring on a bed falls down, it's because one or more of the slats that support it have fallen out of place.

If you look at the slats, you'll likely find one or more bent. What this does, in effect, is to make a shorter slat than originally. The span under the boxspring (from lip to lip on the bed rails) is not covered.

Of course you can probably put back the same slats and support the boxspring for a while. But movement in the bed will eventually work the slats off.

Solve the problem once and for all by replacing the bad slats. Just measure the existing slats and go down to the lumber yard and get ones an inch longer—the lumber-yard will cut the wood to size for you. (Ask for one-by-three boards.) If the slats are too long, just trim them down with a saw until they fit.

Leak in Basement Wall or Floor

On a rainy day, you may notice that a basement wall or floor has some leaks. If this happens, no sweat. There is actually a product that, when applied to a crack or hole from which water is flowing, stops the leak in minutes!

The material is called hydraulic cement. There are various brands. One good one I've used is made by the Rutland Co., of Rutland, Vermont—they call it Hydraulic Cement (of all things).

To use the material to stop a flowing leak, mix it with water until it has the consistency of putty. Wait a few minutes until it stiffens a little. Then, using a trowel or putty knife, force it into the crack or hole and hold it there with the tool for a few minutes until it stays by itself. Add more cement the same way until the water stops flowing. When this occurs, shave the material even with the rest of the wall or floor.

Hydraulic cement is not pretty. It's gray, and the patches will show on the wall or floor. And it's expensive; a 1½-pound can costs around $1.25. But a half hour after you apply it, it will be as hard as a rock, and nary a drop of water in sight. It will look beautiful then.

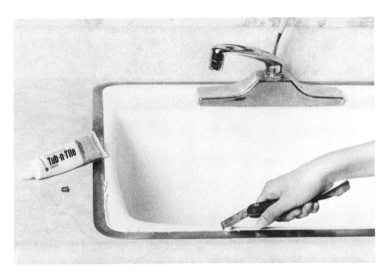

If the joint between a sink and a counter is open, water can get through. Seal it with calk.

Water Leaks Around Kitchen Sink

The way kitchen sinks are set into countertops makes them prone to becoming a little loose. When this occurs, there is space around the sink rim—a perfect place for water to get through.

Solve this problem with the same material used to seal off the joint between the bathtub and the wall—calk. Just fill up the opening around the rim, using a scraper or putty knife. That's it.